BOXING'S SUPER 70'S

Plus

What's Wrong With Boxing's Hall of Fame?

By
Larry Carli

Boxing's Super 70's
Plus: What's Wrong With Boxing's Hall of Fame?

© 2019 Larry Carli

ISBN: 978-1-61170-287-3

Published by:

Rp **Robertson Publishing**™
www.RobertsonPublishing.com

Printed in the USA and UK on acid-free paper.

To purchase additional prints of this book go to:
amazon.com
barnesandnoble.com

Larry Carli has also written:
The Top Ten Middleweight Champions of All Time: Who Was The Greatest?

Foreword

The 1970's brought back the emergence of the super stars of boxing and a return to normalcy from the countries tumultuous 1960's which included the Vietnam War, and political assassinations of John F. Kennedy, Robert Kennedy, and Martin Luther King.

People turned their attention to sports, and cable television brought more boxing into the homes of the average American. Muhammad Ali proved his greatness in the ring in this decade. and it also brought in the emergence of the Latin super stars such as Carlos Monzon, and Roberto Duran.

This book lists the best fighters of the decade in all the major weight divisions, plus a separate section on a list of boxers in each major weight division who have been denied entry into the International Boxing Hall of Fame for various unexplained reasons.

Table of Contents

Table of Contents (cont.)

Table of Contents (cont.)

Muhammad Ali

Photograph from BoxRec

Chapter 1 Top Heavyweights of the Decade

Muhammad Ali

Probably the greatest fighter in the history of the heavyweight division was born Cassius Marcellus Clay on January 17, 1942, in Louisville, Kentucky. The story goes that a Louisville policeman got young Cassius involved in amateur boxing when he reported that his bicycle had been stolen.

Cassius entered the ranks of amateur boxing and won several major national titles in 1958 and 1959. Cassius made it to the United States Olympic boxing trials in 1960 and won the 178 pound division, qualifying him for a berth on the United States Olympic team.

Cassius won the Gold Medal in the 178 pound division of the Rome Olympics in 1960. Young Cassius returned to Louisville an Olympic hero and immediately signed a professional contract with local businessman men who called themselves the Louisville Sporting Group.

Clay made his professional debut on October 29, 1960, and won a 6-round unanimous decision over journeyman Tunney Hunsaker. Clay went undefeated in his first 5 professional fights and then took on knockout artist Lamar Clark in April of 1961. Clay fractured Clarks nose on his way to a 2nd round knockout.

In October of 1961, Clay knocked out former top ten heavyweight contender Alex Miteff. The fight was even until Miteff was stopped in the 7th round. In February of 1962, Clay is dropped for the first time by Sonny Banks. Clay returns the favor and stopped Banks in the 4th round.

Two weeks after the Banks fight, Clay begins predicting the round he will stop opponents by knocking out Don Warner in 4 rounds.

In May of 1962, Cassius faces his first top ten ranked opponent in rugged and rangy Billy Daniels. Cassius predicts Daniels will fall in 5 rounds, but Daniels puts up a tough fight before being stopped in the 7th round due to cuts.

In July of 1962, Cassius predicts he will knock out Argentine Alejandro Lavorante in 5 rounds. Cassius makes his prediction come true with a 5th round stoppage. Cassius has now won 15 straight fights with 12 wins coming by knockout.

Clay keeps predicting his wins accurately as he stops "the Old Mongoose" Archie Moore in 4 rounds in November of 1962, and Charley Powell in 3 rounds in January of 1963. In March of 1963, Cassius takes on top ten ranked heavyweight Doug Jones and predicts a 4-round knockout. Clay not only fails to knock out Jones but he is hard pressed to win an unpopular close unanimous decision.

Clay ventured to England in June of 1963 to take on British Heavyweight Champion Henry Cooper. Cooper drops Cassius with a left hook in the 2nd round, but Cassius catches a break when his boxing glove is ripped and needs to be repaired. Clay clears his head and stops Cooper on cuts in the 5th round. Ringsiders contend that Cassius' trainer Angelo Dundee intentionally ripped Cassius glove to give him time to clear his head after his knockdown.

Cassius is now the top contender to Sonny Liston's heavyweight title but few boxing critics give him much of a chance to defeat the seemingly invincible Liston. The fight is set for February of 1964 in Miami Beach, and Cassius goes into "a crazy act" at the weigh in which many spectators attribute to him being afraid of Liston.

Cassius enters the ring a 7 to 1 underdog and starts the fight dancing around the ring and moving away from Liston's power punches. Cassius proves to be too fast for Liston and his jabs are causing Liston's eyes to swell in the middle of the fight. By the end of the 4th round Cassius begins blinking and claims that some substance has gotten into his eyes. Dundee has to push Cassius out of his corner to fight until his eyes clear up. By the 6th round, Cassius has opened up cuts around Liston's eyes with his jabs and it appears that Liston is tiring. Liston fails to come out of his corner for the 7th round claiming a shoulder injury, and 22-year-old Cassius Clay is the new heavyweight champion of the world.

One week after the fight Cassius announces to the world that he has joined the Black Muslims Faith and has adopted the name of Muhammad Ali.

Now known as Muhammad Ali, he stops Liston in one round in a rematch in Lewiston, Maine in May of 1965. Many ringsiders do not see the punch that knocked Liston out and the press called it "a phantom punch". It appeared to most ringsiders that Liston could have gotten up before the 10-count.

Ali spent the early part of 1965 doing boxing exhibitions until his November title defense against former champion Floyd Patterson. Ali calls Patterson "the rabbit" and taunts him during his 12th round technical knockout of the injured Patterson in their Las Vegas bout.

In 1966, Muhammad makes a total of 5 title defenses. Many boxing critics think that this was Muhammad's greatest year as champion. He decisioned tough Canadian George Chuvalo in March and stopped Henry Cooper in May, Brian London in August, Karl Mildenberger in September, and Cleveland Williams in November. Muhammad was at his best in the Williams fight as he was absolutely perfect in the ring as he utterly destroyed the power punching Williams inside of 3 one sided rounds.

In February of 1967, Muhammad unified the heavyweight title by winning a 15-round unanimous decision over World Boxing Association champion Ernie Terrell. Ali taunted Terrell during the fight as he repeatedly asked him "what's my name" as Terrell had repeatedly referred to him as "Clay" before their fight.

Muhammad make a final defense against perennial top contender Zora Folley in March. Muhammad stopped Folley in the 7th round, and after the fight he refused military induction in Houston, Texas.

Stripped of his title by the boxing organizations, he began making speeches on college campuses as he came out against the Vietnam War. Muhammad became a popular lecturer on the college campuses and a popular figure to the youth of the country during a time of a divided country over the Vietnam War.

Muhammad was inactive in the ring in 1968 and 1969 until he was finally cleared of his draft conviction by the United States Supreme Court. The World Boxing Association initiated a boxing tournament to name a successor to Muhammad's title. Jimmy Ellis, Muhammad's old sparring partner won the tournament in 1968 and was named the World Boxing Association heavyweight champion. Joe Frazier refused to enter the tournament, and he won New York recognition as heavyweight champion when he stopped Buster Mathis in 1968 in Madison Square Garden.

In February of 1970, Frazier stopped Ellis in 5 rounds in New York City in a title unification match. Frazier made several title defenses and waited for Ali's return.

Muhammad finally returned to the ring in October of 1970 in Atlanta, Georgia against top contender Jerry Quarry. Muhammad came out fast in the first round and immediately Quarry suffered a serious eye cut. The fight was finally stopped in the 3rd round due to the eye cut but the fight was too short to accurately assess how rusty Ali had become during his hiatus from the ring.

Muhammad took on rugged Argentine contender Oscar (Ringo) Bonavena in December to determine Joe Frazier's next title challenger. Bonavena proved to be a much stiffer test for Ali then Jerry Quarry. Bonavena took Mohammad's best punches and came back fighting. The fight was still relatively close until the 15th round when Muhammad caught Bonavena coming in with a solid punch knocking him down. Muhammad dropped Bonavena 2 more times in the final round for an automatic 15th round technical knockout win. Muhammad was aided in the stoppage by the referee who did not make him go to a neutral corner after the knockdowns.

The victory over Bonavena set the stage for the Fight of the Century. Muhammad signed to fight Joe Frazier in March of 1971 in Madison Square Garden. Each fighter was to be paid 2.5 million dollars, which was considered an astronomical sum at the time.

Frazier was portrayed by Ali as an "Uncle Tom" and the establishment's champion, where Ali proclaimed himself to be the lineal and peoples champion. Ali entered the ring first, wearing red trunks and red tassels on his white shoes. Frazier entered the ring wearing green paisley trunks.

It was evident from the start that Ali had lost a step as Frazier was able to work the body and reach him with left hooks. Ali's movement and effective jabs kept the fight close until Frazier opened up in the 11th round and nearly knocked Ali out. Frazier dropped Ali with a left hook to the jaw in the 15th round and took the 15-round unanimous decision.

Ali lost no prestige from the fight and came out of it more popular than ever. He boxed exhibitions during the early part of 1971, then beat up on his ex-sparring partner and former World Boxing Association champion Jimmy Ellis in June, and finished out the year winning a decision over huge Buster Mathis and knocking out German Jurgen Blin in 7 rounds in December.

Muhammad won an easy 15-round decision over rated contender Mac Foster in April of 1972, and easily stopped jaded veteran Jerry Quarry in 7 rounds in June of the same year. Muhammad stopped old foe Floyd Patterson in 7 rounds in September, and light heavyweight champion Bob Foster in 8 rounds in November. Foster was able reach Muhammad during the fight and actually cut one of Muhammad's eyes before being stopped.

Muhammad was upset by Ken Norton in March of 1973 and suffered a broken jaw during the fight. Muhammad defeated Norton in a rematch in November, and also defeated Joe Frazier in their rematch in January of 1974. The rematch with Frazier was not a classic as there was a lot of holding and clinching in their fight. Frazier complained after the fight that the referee did not allow any infighting during the match. The Frazier victory set the stage for Muhammad to challenge current world heavyweight champion, George Foreman, to the title in Zaire.

The fight finally took place in October of 1974, as Foreman was cut in training and the fight had to be postponed for a month. The undefeated Foreman was a huge favorite with the odds makers, but Ali was the hometown favorite of the African crowd.

Foreman came out for the first round aggressively, as usual, looking for the knockout. Muhammad would spear Foreman occasionally with straight right hands and generally avoided trouble in the early going. Foreman would follow Muhammad to the ropes and blast away to the body, but Muhammad was catching a lot of the blows on his arms and elbows. Foreman did not pace himself and

6

Muhammad began catching him with occasional jabs and quick right crosses. Foreman's face was starting to puff up, and he was not used to someone fighting back and hanging in there with him. Foreman was swinging wildly trying for the knockout, and was still slightly ahead when Muhammad caught him with a straight right hand in the 8th round that dropped him to the canvas in the middle of the ring. Knocked down and tired, Foreman barely missed beating referee Zack Claytons 10-count. After 7 years Muhammad was again the heavyweight champion of the world in a stunning upset. Ali called his method of laying on the ropes, his "rope-a-dope" method of fighting. Ali explained that it was his method of having Foreman punch himself out during the match.

Muhammad became only the second man to regain the heavyweight championship and he enjoyed worldwide popularity. Muhammad returned to the ring in March of 1975 to stop journeyman Chuck Wepner in the 15th and final round of their title fight. Muhammad suffered a controversial knockdown in this match, and Wepner put up a game but losing battle. It was later reported the movie ROCKY in 1976 was based upon the Ali vs. Wepner fight.

In May, Muhammad stopped Ron Lyle in 11 rounds of a close title fight on the scorecards and decisioned England's Joe Bugner in a July title defense. In October of 1975, Muhammad took on Joe Frazier in their rubber match in Manila.

The rubber match was a boxing classic between two great heavyweights in the twilight of their careers. Muhammad started off fast, boxing and moving, but Frazier came on strong in the middle rounds with a vicious body attack. The two fighters fought with every ounce of their strength until Frazier was unable to see and come out for the 15th and final round.

Muhammad said after the fight that he felt like quitting, and it was the closest thing he ever felt to death in the ring. In February of 1976, Muhammad made an easy title defense by stopping Jean

Pierre Coopman in 5 rounds, and in April he won a 15-round decision over top contender Jimmy Young. Muhammad won the unanimous decision, but he did not look good in defeating Young. It appeared that if Young had been more aggressive that he may have been able to win the fight over the lethargic champion.

Muhammad stopped overmatched contender Richard Dunn in May, and took on Ken Norton in their rubber match in September in Madison Square Garden. Muhammad was given a close 15-round decision, but many ringsiders felt that Norton had actually won the fight. Muhammad always appeared to have trouble with Norton's style of fighting and cross arm defense.

Muhammad boxed a series of exhibitions in the early part of 1977 and finally made a title defense against Spaniard Alfredo Evangelista in May. Muhammad took an easy 15-round decision over Evangelista and then took on dangerous punching Earnie Shavers in September. Shavers rocked Muhammad on several occasions during the fight, but Muhammad was able to stay out of danger on his way to a unanimous decision in a competitive fight.

Muhammad took on Olympic Heavyweight Gold Medalist Leon Spinks in February of 1978. Spinks had only been fighting professional for one year and had only 7 professional fights when he challenged Muhammad. Spinks won a 15-round decision over an out of shape and listless Muhammad. It appeared that Muhammad had finally reached the end of his boxing career, but a rematch was set for September in New Orleans.

Muhammad showed up for the rematch in shape and took Spinks seriously this time. Muhammad won a 15-round decision over Spinks to become the first heavyweight to win the championship 3 times.

Muhammad should have probably retired after the Spinks fight, and he did not fight in 1979. In 1980, Muhammad made an ill-advised comeback and took a severe beating from Larry Holmes as he was stopped in the 11th round of a one-sided fight. This was the first time that Muhammad had been stopped in his entire professional career.

Muhammad fought one last time in 1981 and lost a drab 10-round decision to contender Trevor Berbick in the Bahamas. Muhammad retired with a final ring record of 56 wins, and 5 losses. He won 37 fights by knockout.

Muhammad was aptly nicknamed 'The Greatest" and he probably was the greatest heavyweight champion of all time, and most certainly the greatest heavyweight of the 1960s and 1970s. He was certainly the most charismatic heavyweight champion and he was adored by people all over the world.

Even the greatest professional fighters do not remain unscathed fighting for over 20 years in the ring. Sacramento, California board certified Sports Medicine Doctor Rita B. Bermudez stated that repeated blows to the brain cause small hemorrhages, inflammation, and metabolic dysfunction that leaves neurons vulnerable to stress and genetic factors. This can lead to the premature loss of nerve cells, including those associated with Parkinson's disease. Dr. Bermudez also reported that researchers at Arizona State University analyzed Ali's speech during taped interviews and noted a 26 per cent decrease in his rate of speech from 1968 to 1981. They also found an association between Ali's range in vocal pitch and loudness and the number of days since his last fight. In particular there was a 15 per cent decrease in Ali's rate of speech after his fight with Ernie Shavers in 1977, when he took 266 punches. Since slowing of speech is an early sign of Parkinson's this certainly suggests that boxing played an important role in Ali's development of Parkinson's[1].

Muhammad Ali was one of the first fighters to be inducted into the International Boxing Hall of Fame, class of 1990. Sadly, after suffering from the dreaded Parkinson's disease for over 30 years, Muhammed passed away at the age of 74 in the year 2016.

---

[1] Berisha, Visar & Liss, Julie & Huston, Timothy & Wisler, Alan & Jiao, Yishan & Eig, Jonathan. (1970). Float Like a Butterfly Sting Like a Bee: Changes in Speech Preceded Parkinsonism Diagnosis for Muhammad Ali. 1809-1813. 10.21437/Interspeech.2017-25.

George Foreman

Photograph from BoxRec

George Foreman

George Foreman was born on January 10, 1949, in Marshall, Texas. George joined the Job Corps as a youth and began an amateur boxing career in the Bay Area of California under the guidance of Dick Sadler. George became famous for winning the Gold Medal in the heavyweight division at the 1968 Olympics and carrying an American flag around the ring after his final bout.

At 6-3 in height, and a solid 220 pounds, George was a powerhouse of a heavyweight. George turned professional after the Olympics in June of 1969 when he knocked out Don Waldheim in 3 rounds. George had the advantage of having former Featherweight Champion Sandy Saddler in his corner, and he was brought along very slowly in his early career.

George won all 13 of his fights in 1969, with 11 wins coming by knockout. Only Roberto Davila, and Levi Forte were able to take a severe beating and still go the distance with big George. The only name opponent that George beat in 1969 was Chuck Wepner.

George won all 12 of his fights in 1970, and only former light heavyweight contender Gregorio Peralta was able to go the distance with him. Among George's kayo victims in 1970 was top ranked heavyweight George Chuvalo who was kayoed in 3 rounds.

George won all 7 of his fights in 1971 and knocked out Gregorio Peralta in a rematch of their 1970 fight. George entered the top ten heavyweight rankings, and after he knocked out all 5 of his opponents in 1972, he became the top ranked contender for Joe Frazier's heavyweight title.

George challenged Frazier for the title in January of 1973 in Kingston, Jamaica. George entered the ring with a record of 37-0 with 34 wins coming by knockout. Most experts dismissed George as just a crude slugger, who for the most part fought a bunch of over the hill heavyweight contenders. It was felt that Frazier was too polished and experienced for the young challenger to handle.

When the two heavyweights stepped into the ring in Jamaica, the size difference was apparent. George at 6-3 in height towered over the 5-11-inch champion. George had Dick Sadler, Sandy Saddler, and the Old Mongoose, Archie Moore, in his corner. Frazier's style of aggressive fighting was made to order for the powerful young challenger

At the bell for round one when Frazier came in close, George pushed him away and belted him with both hands to the head and body. George's uppercuts were literally lifting Frazier off of the ground. Frazier was dropped a total of 6 times and was stopped in the 2nd round of the one-sided contest.

George made his first title defense against number one contender Ken Norton in March of 1974 in Caracas, Venezuela. Norton appeared to freeze up in the fight, and a shell-shocked Norton was knocked out by George in the 2nd round of another one-sided fight.

In October of 1974, George was challenged by former champion Muhammad Ali in a match for the title in Zaire, Africa. The match was promoted by Don King. George suffered a severe cut in training and the match had to be postponed for a month. George entered the ring in Africa, somewhat ill prepared for the match and appeared to be bothered by the pro-Ali crowds.

George started off in his usual aggressive manner, but Ali danced around the ring and then would back into the ropes, and let George wail away aimlessly at his head and body. Ali would come off of the ropes and fight in spurts with counter punches to keep the fight competitive. George kept after Ali in the fight but he was not pacing himself and began to tire in the middle rounds. In the 8th round Ali caught George with a straight right hand to the head which dropped the exhausted champion flat on his back in the middle of the ring. George got up but just missed beating referee Zack Clayton's 10-count, and Ali became a two-time heavyweight champion.

George returned to the United States an ex-champion and stayed out of the ring until April of 1975 when he boxed 3-round exhibition matches with 5 different fighters in Toronto, Canada. The exhibition matches took on somewhat of a circus atmosphere and actually did some damage to George's reputation as a serious contender.

In January of 1976, George took on another power puncher in heavyweight contender Ron Lyle. The match was held in Las Vegas and it won fight of the year honors. Both fighters hit the canvas on several occasions before Lyle finally took the 10-count in the 5th round. The bout was a fight fans dream as the fighters just took turns belting each other around the ring before Lyle finally caved in. Neither fighter showed much boxing skill before George finally overpowered Lyle to win the fight.

In June of 1976, George gave Joe Frazier a rematch in Uniondale, New York. Frazier was more cautious in the rematch, and lasted until the 5th round before George finally caught up to him and stopped him. George finished out the year by stopping trial horses Scott LeDoux and John (Dino) Dennis.

In January of 1977, George stopped Pedro Agosto and then took on top ranked Jimmy Young in Puerto Rico in March. George started off strong, and dropped Young in the middle rounds. Young was an experienced boxer, and he avoided most of George's big punches and actually dropped George in the last round to take a 12-round decision.

George suffered from heat exhaustion after the fight, and claimed that he saw a vision from God and then abruptly retired from the ring. George became a preacher in Texas and stayed out of the ring for 10 years. George returned to the ring in 1987, and claimed that he was making a comeback to help support his Christian Youth Groups.

George made his return to the ring in Sacramento, California in 1987, and looked ponderous and slow in knocking out journeyman heavyweight Steve Zouski in 4 rounds. George had lost a lot of his mobility, but retained most of his punching power.

George won all 9 of his fights in 1988, including a win over former light heavyweight, and cruiserweight champion Dwight Muhammed Qawi. George appeared more relaxed in his comeback fights and he had a more jovial personality then the moody serious-minded fighter that he was in the 1970's.

In 1989 George knocked out heavyweight contender Bert Cooper, and in January of 1990, he took on former heavyweight top contender Gerry Cooney in a battle of sluggers. Cooney wobbled George with left hooks in the first round, but George survived the round and came back to knock Cooney out in the second round.

After a few more knockout wins, George challenged Evander Holyfield for the heavyweight title in April of 1991. George rocked Holyfield on several occasions, but could not catch him with a knockout punch. Holyfield won a unanimous decision over George to hold on to the belt.

In June of 1993, George took on Tommy Morrison for the vacant World Boxing Organization title belt. Morrison boxed carefully and mixed in some power punches to gain the decision over George in his second attempt at winning back the heavyweight belt.

In November of 1994, George took on World Boxing Association champion Michael Moorer in another attempt to win a heavyweight championship. Moorer was a young powerful champion who had once held a light heavyweight championship belt. Moorer out boxed George for the first 9 rounds, but George kept plodding forwarded with a puffed face from Moorer's powerful jabs. Finally, in the 10th round, George saw the opening he had been waiting for, and launched a straight right hand to Moorer's jaw. The blow knocked Moorer flat onto his back for the 10-count.

At the age of 45, George became the oldest heavyweight champion in history and capped an incredible 7-year comeback to obtain the title. In 1995, George defended his International Boxing Federation belt against German Axel Schulz. Schulz put up a terrific battle, and George was lucky to escape with a majority decision.

In 1996, George defended what was left of his title recognition to defeat Crawford Grimsley by a 12-round decision. In 1997, George defended his lineal heavyweight championship against Lou Savarese and won a hard-fought split decision.

In 1997, George lost his lineal title in a highly disputed majority decision to Shannon Briggs. George rocked Briggs repeatedly during the fight, but somehow the judges felt that Briggs had done enough to win the fight.

George retired after the Briggs fight with a final ring record of 76 wins, and 5 losses. He won 68 fights by knockout. After the Briggs fight George became a television boxing analyst for HBO. George was inducted into the International Boxing Hall of Fame in 2003 and has made over 200 million dollars in endorsements of his

George Foreman grill, and other products. His popularity today is rivaled only by former 3-time world champion Muhammad Ali.

Joe Frazier

Photograph from BoxRec

Joe Frazier

"Smokin Joe" Frazier was born on January 10, 1944, in Beaufort, South Carolina. Joe did farm work as a youth and eventually relocated to Philadelphia, Pennsylvania. Joe took up amateur boxing and made the 1964 United States Olympic boxing team as an alternate

When heavyweight Buster Mathis injured his hand in training, Joe replaced him on the Olympic boxing team and won the Gold Medal in the heavyweight division of the 1964 summer games.

Yancey "Yank" Durham trained Joe, and a group of local Philadelphia businessmen put together a group called "Cloverlay" to invest in his professional boxing career. Durham taught Joe his bob and weave style of fighting and to always move forward throwing his famous left hook.

Joe turned professional in August of 1965 and won all 4 of his fights that year by knockout. Joe won his first 7 fights by knockout in 1966, and then he met rugged Argentine Oscar (Ringo) Bonavena in September. Bonavena dropped Joe twice in one round during the fight and Joe barely escaped with an unpopular split decision win.

In November, Joe knocked out former heavyweight top contender Eddie Machen in 10 rounds, and then stopped George Chuvalo in 4 rounds in July of 1967. Muhammad Ali was stripped of his title in 1967 for refusing induction into military service, and Joe fought former amateur opponent Buster Mathis in March of 1968 for the New York version of the heavyweight title. Joe gained revenge for his amateur defeat by stopping Mathis in 11 rounds to claim New York's version of the heavyweight title. Jimmy Ellis won the World Boxing Association version of the heavyweight title when he won a decision over Jerry Quarry in April of 1968.

Joe defended his title twice in 1968, knocking out Manuel Ramos in 2 rounds in June, and winning a hard fought 15-round unanimous decision over Oscar Bonavena in December.

Joe kept Bonavena pinned on the ropes for the majority of the fight and gave him very little punching room during the fight. Joe opened 1969 by knocking out unknown Dave Zyglewicz in one round in April, and then sliced up and stopped previous top contender Jerry Quarry in 7 rounds of non-stop action.

Jimmy Ellis had defended his World Boxing Association title in 1968 by winning an unpopular 15-round decision over former champion Floyd Patterson in Sweden, and a unification match with Joe was set for February of 1970 in Madison Square Garden.

Ellis started out the unification match fast and won the first two rounds with his boxing skills. Joe started coming on in the third round and started landing his left hook to slow Ellis down. By the fourth round Ellis was in severe trouble and the fight was stopped in the 5th round after Ellis had been dropped and was in no shape to continue the battle.

Joe made a defense of his title against Light Heavyweight Champion Bob Foster in Detroit in November. Foster was too strong for the light heavyweights, but his punches did not appear to have any effect on Joe and he was stopped in the second round by a devastating left hook to the head.

Joe's victory over Foster set the stage for his "fight of the century" against the former and lineal heavyweight champion,

Muhammad Ali. Ali had returned to the ring in 1970 and had stopped Jerry Quarry in 3 rounds and Oscar Bonavena in 15 rounds to qualify for his title challenge.

Ali considered himself "the peoples champion" and painted Frazier as 'the establishment" champion to the press. Joe was made a slight favorite in the fight due to Ali's period of inactivity. Each fighter was to be paid 2.5 million dollars for the fight, which was an astronomical sum of money in 1971. The match was finally set for March 8, 1971, in Madison Square Garden.

Ali entered the ring, and appeared loose and confident in his corner. Frazier entered the ring, and appeared to have a stoic look on his face, and seemed anxious for the fight to start. The bell rang, and Ali came out flicking jabs, while Frazier followed him around the ring. Ali danced around the ring throwing an occasional right hand, while Frazier largely just posed.

It appeared that Ali won the first couple of rounds, but Joe began to reach him in the third round with left hooks to the head and body. Frazier picked up the pace, and matched Ali punch for punch as the fight entered into the middle rounds. It was obvious this was going to be an evenly contested fight.

Ali clowned during the fight, and this may have cost him couple of the middle rounds. The fight was still close after 10 rounds, but Joe nearly knocked Ali out in the 11th round and Ali was in serious trouble when the bell rang ending the round.

Joe continued his attack in the 12th, and 13th rounds, but Ali fought hard and took the 14th round. Joe landed a monstrous left hook to the head in the 15th round to drop Ali flat on his back near a corner. Ali gamely got up with a swollen jaw and fought back until the end of the fight.

The fight was a classic between two great fighters, and Joe was given a well-deserved unanimous decision. If anything, Ali gained more popularity with his game effort after a 3 year layoff from the ring.

Joe boxed a couple of exhibitions during the rest of the year and did not defend his title until January of 1972, when he stepped into the ring against Terry Daniels in New Orleans. Joe stopped the relatively unknown Daniels in 4 rounds, and then took on another unknown in Ron Stander in May. Joe chopped up Stander's face for an easy technical knockout victory in 4 rounds.

Joe's next opponent would be the undefeated former heavyweight Olympic champion George Foreman. Foreman was undefeated as a professional in 37 fights, but he was considered too crude and relatively untested to take Joe's title. The fight was set for January of 1973, and it was to be held in Kingston, Jamaica.

When the fighters entered the ring, the size difference was apparent. Foreman at 6-3 in height towered over the 5-11-inch champion. The obnoxious Howard Cosell was the nationwide announcer for the closed-circuit broadcast. Joe started the fight by charging straight at the powerful Foreman. Joe's style of fighting was ready made for Foreman. Foreman did not have to go looking for Joe as the champion walked right into his power. Foreman's powerful blows literally lifted Joe right off of the canvas into a second round defeat. Cosell kept screaming to the audience "down goes Frazier, down goes Frazier" as the fight progressed. Joe's corner threw in the towel in the 2nd round of a one-sided beat down.

Joe did not fight again until July when he went to England and won a 12-round decision over British contender Joe Bugner. Joe showed flashes of his old brilliance in the match but he was not able to come close to stopping the British heavyweight.

In January of 1974, Joe took on Muhammad Ali in a rematch. Joe lost the match but it was far from a classic. The match was marred by frequent clinching, and Joe complained later that the referee allowed Ali to hold him during the match and that he was prevented from infighting. The match proved that Joe had lost a step inside of the ring.

Joe returned to action in June and continued his dominance of Jerry Quarry by stopping the perennial contender in 5 rounds of their New York rematch. In March of 1975, Joe traveled to Melbourne, Australia to fight a rematch with Jimmy Ellis. Ellis boxed cautiously and was able to last until the 9th round before Joe caught up to him and stopped him

Ali was still the champion after stopping Foreman in Africa in 1974, and their rubber match was set for October of 1975 in Manila. This may have been the last great fight for both warriors. Both fighters went all out in every round with Ali's jabs puffing up and closing Frazier's eyes. Frazier did terrible damage to Ali with his vicious body attack in the middle rounds. Ali survived Joe's body attack and came back to stop him when Joe was unable to see and come out for the 15th and last round. Both fighters gave it all they had, and they had nothing left at the end of the fight.

In June of 1976, Joe shaved his head and fought a return match with George Foreman in Uniondale, New York. Joe took a more cautious approach in the rematch, and he was able to box and move and counterpunch until he was stopped in the 5th round by Foreman's power punches.

Joe retired after the Foreman rematch, and then made an ill-advised comeback when he took on Floyd "Jumbo" Cummings, a rough and tumble muscular graduate of the prison system. Joe was well past his prime, but he still had enough power left to hold the younger Cummings to a draw. Joe retired for good after the Cummings fight with a final ring record of 32 wins, 4 losses, and 1 draw. Joe won 27 fights by knockout, mostly with his vicious left hooks. The only two men who ever defeated Joe were Muhammad Ali and George Foreman.

The names Ali and Frazier will always be linked in boxing history. To build up their fights to the press, and to the public, Ali frequently insulted Joe and called him "a gorilla" and portrayed him to the press as "Uncle Tom" and an establishment fighter. Joe was deeply offended by Ali's remarks and took them personally. Writer Bryant Gumbel even wrote an article in a Boxing Illustrated magazine asking if Joe Frazier was a white champion in black skin

The animosity lingered for years between the two fighters, and not until their declining years were any attempts made by them to reconcile their differences. Unlike Foreman and Ali who became financially secure from boxing, it has been reported that Joe suffered from financial problems in retirement due to bad business investments and his generosity to friends.

It has been said that without his rivalry with Joe Frazier, Ali would not have been as popular as he was, and the two great warriors gave fight fans two of the greatest fights of the decade.

Joe spent his retirement traveling around Europe, and singing with his musical group Joe Frazier and the Knockouts. Joe also trained his son Marvis Frazier when he turned professional, and owned and managed a gym in his hometown of Philadelphia. Joe was inducted into the International Boxing Hall of Fame in 1990.

Joe passed away from liver cancer in 2011 at the age of 67. His longtime rival Muhammad Ali was in attendance at the funeral.

Bob Foster

Photograph from BoxRec

Chapter 2 Top Light Heavyweights of the Decade

Bob Foster

Robert Lloyd Foster, known to the boxing world simply as Bob Foster, was born on December 1, 1938, in Borger, Texas. At 6-3 in height, Bob turned professional as a light heavyweight on March 27, 1961, by stopping Duke Williams in 2 rounds in Washington D.C.

Bob won all 7 of his fights in 1961, and 5 wins were by knockout. Bob alternated fighting between the light heavyweight and heavyweight divisions in 1962, and he defeated Billy Tisdale, and veteran Bert Whitehurst before being stopped by heavyweight contender Doug Jones in October.

Bob won his first two fights by knockout in 1963 before he traveled to Lima, Peru in November and lost a disputed decision to local favorite Mauro Mina. Bob returned to the USA in December and stopped heavyweight trial horse Willie Besmanoff in 3 rounds.

Bob won 5 of his 6 fights in 1964. He stopped top light heavyweights Allen Thomas in May and Henry Hank in December. His only losing effort was when he was stopped by Ernie (Terrible) Terrell in 7 rounds in July. Bob was too strong for his light heavyweight competition, but he did not seem to be able to take a punch from the top heavyweight contenders.

Bob defeated Henry Hank again in a rematch in July of 1965 to gain a top ten ranking in the light heavyweight division but, when he took on top heavyweight competition in the form of Zora Folley in December, he suffered another loss.

Bob knocked out veteran Eddie Cotton in 3 rounds in Washington D.C. in May of 1967 to become the number one light heavyweight contender to Champion Dick Tiger. Bob finally got his chance at the title when he took on Tiger in May of 1968, in New York

Bob had over a 6-inch height advantage over the 5-8-inch-tall Tiger and a substantial reach advantage as well. Tiger looked like a midget in the ring standing next to Bob during the pre-fight instructions. Bob boxed patiently for the first 3 rounds before he landed a perfect left hook to Tigers chin in the 4th round. Tiger landed flat on his back, out cold to the world. Bob's first defense was against New Jersey brawler Frank DePaula in January of 1969. Bob suffered a flash knockdown in the 1st round before he came back to drop DePaula several times and stop him in the same round.

In May of 1969, Bob stopped rugged contender Andy Kendall in 4 rounds of a Springfield, Massachusetts title defense. In April of 1970, Bob traveled to Missoula, Montana to take on local light heavyweight contender Roger Rouse. Bob had previously knocked out Rouse in 1968, and he knocked him out again in 4 rounds in this title defense.

In June of 1970, Bob took on Texan Mark Tessman in a Baltimore, Maryland title defense. Tessman was an accomplished boxer and he stayed away from Bob's power for the first 9 rounds. In the 10th round, Bob caught up to the tiring Tessman and stopped him.

In November of 1970, Bob challenged Joe Frazier for the heavyweight title in Detroit, Michigan. Bob's power did not seem to have any effect at all on Joe and he was easily stopped in the 2nd round by smoking Joe's vicious left hooks.

Bob wisely returned to the light heavyweight division and made 4 successful defenses of his title. In March, Bob knocked out Hal Carroll, and won a 15-round decision from a backpedaling frightened contender in Ray Anderson in April. Bob stopped Tommy Hicks in 8 rounds in October, and stopped Brian Kelly in 3 rounds in December.

For some unknown reason, the World Boxing Association, stripped Bob of his title recognition and named Venezuelan Vicente Rondon as their champion after Rondon stopped Jimmy Dupree in February of 1971, in Caracas, Venezuela.

The title unification match was held in Miami Beach, Florida in April of 1972. Bob knocked out a frightened Rondon in the 2nd round in a one-sided beat down. Next up for Bob was undefeated light heavyweight top contender Mike Quarry.

The fight was held in June of 1972, in Las Vegas. Quarry boxed carefully in the first 3 rounds and stayed away from Bob's power. Quarry was knocked cold during an exchange of left hooks in the 4th round, and, like Dick Tiger before him, he did not move during the 10 count while lying flat on his back in the middle of the ring.

Bob's power at the light heavyweight limit was frightening, and in September of 1972 he traveled to London to take on British top contender Chris Finnegan. Finnegan put up a stout challenge and even exchanged power punches with Bob before he was ultimately stopped in the 14th round of the title fight. The Finnegan title defense had proved to be Bob's toughest title challenge since he won the title in 1968.

Bob decided to test the elite fighters in the heavyweight division one last time when he signed to challenge Muhammad Ali in Stateline, Nevada in November of 1972. Bob was actually able to reach Ali with some power punches and cut one of his eyes during the course of the bout. Ali finally put several combinations together and stopped Bob in the 8th round of the fight.

In April of 1973, Bob traveled to South Africa to defend his title against local fighter Pierre Fourie. During the weigh in Bob mistakenly thought Fourie referred to him as "boy" when Fourie actually called him "bob" in his South African accent. Bob was angry from the weigh in incident and punished Fourie for 15 one-sided rounds to win the unanimous decision. This fight was the first mixed race title fight in South African boxing history.

In December of 1973, Bob traveled back to South Africa to offer Fourie a rematch. The rematch was closer, but Bob still won a convincing decision over the determined challenger. Bob's final title defense was set for June of 1974, in his hometown of Albuquerque, New Mexico.

Bob defended his title against Argentine contender Jorge Ahumada in front of his hometown fans. Ahumada was aggressive during the match, and Bob appeared lethargic and unable to land any combinations on the challenger. Bob was lucky to get a draw verdict from the hometown officials and keep his title.

Bob relinquished his title, and retired after the match. Bob's retirement lasted one year before he returned to the ring to knock out Bill Hardney in June of 1975. Bob won 3 fights by knockout in 1976 and one fight by knockout in 1977.

In February of 1978, Bob was stopped by undefeated Ugandan Mustapha Wassaja in Copenhagen in 5 rounds. Bob retired for good when he was stopped in a rematch with Bob Hazelton in 2 rounds in June of 1978.

After retirement Bob returned to Albuquerque to become a deputy sheriff, and detective. Bob will go down in history as one of the biggest punchers in the light heavyweight division. Bob's final ring record was 56 wins, 8 losses, and 1 draw. Bob won 46 fights by knockout.

Bob was inducted into the International Boxing Hall of Fame in 1990. Bob passed away at the age of 76 in 2015.

Victor Galindez

Photograph from Guantes, May 1978

Victor Galindez

Victor Emilio Galindez was born in Buenos Aires, Argentina on November 2, 1948. As an amateur he participated in the 1968 Summer Olympics. He won a silver medal in the Pan American games earlier in 1967.

Victor turned professional in May of 1969 with a 4th round knockout over Ramon Ruiz. By his third fight he was fighting in 10-round bouts and was held to a draw by Adolfo Cejas.

Victor suffered his first defeat in his 6th professional fight when he lost a 10-round decision to tough Juan Aguilar. In 1970, Victor drew, and lost to, Juan Aguilar in rematches, and also lost to Avenamar Peralta in a bid for the Argentine light heavyweight title.

In 1971, Victor was able to knockout arch rival Jorge Ahumada twice, and win a decision over old nemesis Juan Aguilar. In December, Victor again lost a decision to Avenamar Peralta. In January of 1972, Victor knocked out Carlos Santagada in 9 rounds to begin an undefeated streak of 43 bouts over the next 6 years.

Victor finally won the Argentine light heavyweight title when he won a 12-round decision over old foe Juan Aguilar in July of 1972. Victor also won the South American light heavyweight title in September with a 12-round decision over Avenamar Peralta.

In 1973, Victor defeated top contender Eddie Owens, and defended his Argentine light heavy weight title with a 12-round decision over Raul Loyola. In February of 1974, Victor defeated top light heavyweight contender Ray Anderson and World champion Bob Foster retired in September of the same year leaving the title vacant. The World Boxing Council ordered John Conteh to fight Jorge Ahumada for their version of the world title while the World Boxing Association named Victor and Detroit's Len Hutchins as their top contenders for the world title.

Victor fought Hutchins for the vacant World Boxing Association belt in December of 1974, in Buenos Aires. Victor used an aggressive counter punching style of offense to totally overwhelm Hutchins and stop him in the 13th round to gain the World Boxing Association title.

Prior to winning the championship, Victor had not fought outside of Argentina, but that was about to change once he was champion. In April of 1975, Victor traveled to South Africa to defend against perennial contender Pierre Fourie. Victor won a convincing 15-round decision over the South African.

In May, Victor fought in the United States for the first time when he stopped Ray J. Elson in Las Vegas in a non-title fight. Victor then defended his title against countryman Jorge Ahumada in New York, in June. Victor won a 15-round decision in a hard fought competitive fight. Victor helped his cause by hitting Ahumada after the bell in the middle of the fight. Ahumada did not appear to totally recover from the after the bell punch.

As champion, Victor was becoming a world traveler as he returned to South Africa in September to win another 15-round decision over Pierre Fourie in a rematch of their April fight. Fourie lost a total of 4 world title matches during his career.

In March of 1976, Victor knocked out Richie Kates in the 15th and final round of a close bloody fight. Victor suffered some severe facial cuts during the Kates fight which would affect him the rest of his career.

Victor had become somewhat of a fan favorite in South Africa, and he returned there to defend against local contender Kosie Smith. Victor defended his title with another 15-round decision over a local fighter.

Richie Kates had demanded a rematch of their first fight, and Victor's title defense was set for Rome, Italy in June of 1977. Victor won a unanimous decision over Kates in the rematch. Victor did not need a last round knockout to successfully defend his title this time.

Victor defended his title twice more in 1977 with decisions over Yaqui Lopez in September and Eddie Mustapha Muhammad in November in Turin, Italy. The Mustapha Muhammad fight was very close, and Victor was lucky to hang on to his title against the seemingly uninspired challenger.

In May of 1978, Victor defeated Yaqui Lopez in a rematch of their 1977 fight. Victor escaped with another close decision win.

Victor's luck in the ring finally ran out when Mike Rossman stopped him in the 13th round in their September title fight in New Orleans on the Muhammad Ali vs. Leon Spinks fight card. It was thought after the Rossman loss that Victor would retire

Instead of retiring, Victor returned to the ring in March of 1979, and knocked out Roberto Aguilar in 7 rounds. Victor then challenged Rossman again for the title in April in New Orleans. Victor fought an inspired fight and shocked Rossman by knocking him out in 10 rounds to regain his light heavyweight title.

Victor lost his title again when Marvin Johnson knocked him out in 11 rounds in New Orleans. In June of 1980, Victor lost a 12-

round decision to Jessie Burnett in Anaheim, California, and retired from the ring.

After retirement, Victor pursued his passion of auto racing, but tragically he was killed during one of his races in Argentina in October of 1980, at the age of 31. Victors final ring record was 55 wins, 9 losses, and 4 draws. He won 34 fights by knockout.

While Bob Foster dominated the light heavyweight division during the first half of the decade, Victor certainly dominated the division during the second half of the decade even though he was never to obtain a match with John Conteh to unify the title. Victor was inducted into the International Boxing Hall of Fame in 2002.

John Conteh

Photograph from BoxRec

John Conteh

John Anthony Conteh was born on May 27, 1951, in Liverpool, Lancashire, England to an Irish mother and father from Sierra Leone.

John began boxing at age 11, and at age 19 he won the middleweight gold medal at the 1970 British Commonwealth games. John won approximately 46 out of 50 amateur fights.

John turned professional in October of 1971, and knocked out Okacha Boubekeur in one round. John fought as a heavyweight, even though he rarely weighed more than 182 pounds, and won his first 10 fights until he lost a points decision to American veteran Eddie Duncan.

John won his next 6 fights behind his educated left jab and hook. In March of 1973, John dropped down to the light heavyweight division to challenge European Champion Rudiger Schmidtke for the title. Schmidtke had knocked out British Commonwealth Champion Chris Finnegan for the title and was considered a rising star in the light heavyweight division.

John out boxed and out fought Schmidtke throughout the fight before he stopped him in the 12th round to take the light heavyweight European title. In May, John defended his European title against Commonwealth champion Finnegan. John proved he was the best light heavyweight in England as he won a convincing

15-round decision to take Finnegan's British and Commonwealth titles as well.

In September, John knocked out former World Boxing Association champion Vicente Rondon in 9 rounds in London. In October, John defended his Commonwealth light heavyweight title against Baby Boy Rolle in Nottingham, England. John boxed superbly in taking a unanimous decision.

At this point in his career, it seemed like John had to fight every two months to either defend his European light heavyweight title or his Commonwealth light heavyweight title. In March of 1974, fighting on a regular basis, John stopped Denmark's Tom Bogs to defend his European belt, and in May he stopped Chris Finnegan in a rematch to defend the European and Commonwealth title.

Lineal light heavyweight champion Bob Foster announced his retirement in September, and John was immediately matched with Argentine Jorge Ahumada for the World Boxing Council's version of the title. The title match was set for October 1st in London. Ahumada had held Foster to a controversial draw in June before Foster had retired. Many ringsiders felt that Ahumada actually deserved the decision.

John out boxed Ahumada at long range and matched him punch for punch during the fight at close quarters. John won a well-deserved, and hard fought, decision from the official in the fight to take the World Boxing Council version of the light heavyweight title. In a tough fight, the pride of England had come through, and the handsome Conteh was the star of British boxing.

After basking in the limelight for close to six months, John finally signed to defend his title against American challenger Lonnie Bennett in March of 1975, in London. Bennett was an accomplished boxer and promised to give John a stiff test. John proved to be too fast and powerful for Bennett and stopped him in the 5th round in front of an adoring and screaming crowd.

John's manager, George Francis, called for a showdown with World Boxing Association Champion Victor Galindez who had stopped Len Hutchins in December of 1974. Unfortunately, the World Boxing Association and World Boxing Council showed no interest in unifying the title as they wished to protect their own interests and sanctioning fees.

In August John traveled to Scranton, Pennsylvania and took on journeyman Willie Taylor in a 10 round non-title fight. John won a unanimous decision over Taylor, but it proved to be a very costly win. John broke his hand in the fight, and had to fight the second half of the fight with one hand. The break in John's hand was severe and he was on the shelf for over a year.

John returned to the ring in October of 1976 to defend his title against perennial contender Alvaro (Indian Yaqui) Lopez in Copenhagen, Denmark. John shook off his ring rust, to pepper Lopez with left jabs, hooks, and occasional right hands to pound out a unanimous decision over the tough challenger.

John defended his belt for the third time when he defended against Len Hutchins in front of his hometown crowd in Liverpool, England. John was at his devastating best when he stopped Hutchins in 3 rounds. Unfortunately, at this point in his career John began experiencing managerial problems over finance and contract issues.

John was stripped of his title by the World Boxing Council in May of 1977 for failing to go through with a title defense against Miguel Angel Cuello of Argentina. Boxing injuries, contract disputes over television rights, and managerial issues kept John from following through on his title fight commitments.

John returned to the ring in February of 1978 to win a 10-round decision over Joe Cokes. John then signed to meet current World Boxing Council Champion Mate Parlov in what was then called Yugoslavia. The match was held in June of 1978 in Belgrade. John felt that he did enough to win the decision but Parlov was given the verdict in his own hometown in a very close fight.

John tried to regain his title again, but was decisioned by Matthew Saad Muhammad in an August of 1979 title fight. It was later discovered that Saad Muhammad had used an illegal substance on his eye injuries, and John was given a rematch.

The rematch took place in Atlantic City, New Jersey in May of 1980. John did not put up much of a fight and he was stopped in the 3rd round. John retired on a winning note when he stopped James Dixon in 5 rounds in front of his fans in Liverpool in May of 1980

After retirement, John had to battle alcoholism for several years. John was eventually able to overcome his alcohol issues and become a regular after dinner speaker on the Sport and Dinner circuit in England.

John has acted in several movies and got involved with helping various charities in England. In 2017, John was appointed Member of the Order of the British Empire (MBE) for services to boxing. John's final ring record was 34 wins, 4 losses, and 1 draw. He won 24 fights by knockout. Had it not been for his boxing injuries and managerial problems, it is hard to say how great John could have really been. Unfortunately, a much anticipated title unification match with then World Boxing Association Champion Victor Galindez never materialized due to the politics of the various sanctioning boxing bodies.

Carlos Monzon

Photograph from BoxRec

Chapter 3 Top Middleweights of the Decade

Carlos Monzon

Carlos Monzon was born on August 7, 1942, in Santa Fe, Argentina. Carlos came from the farm frontier provinces of Argentina and was dirt poor as a youth. Carlos made money by wining street fights, got into trouble with the law for starting a riot at a soccer game, and he was also accused of running a string of prostitutes before he began his boxing career.

Carlos eventually went to a gym to take up amateur boxing and met his future father figure in his trainer and manager, Amilcar Brusa. Brusa turned Carlos professional in 1963 when he turned 20 years of age. Carlos defeated Ramon Montenegro in 4 rounds in February, and by his 4th professional fight, he was fighting in 10 round bouts.

In Carlos' first year of professional boxing he won 9 out of 10 fights, losing only to the more experienced Antonio Aguilar. In 1964, Carlos fought 11 times, winning 8 matches, losing 2, and fighting 1 draw. His only losses were to Felipe Cambeiro in Rio de Janeiro in June and to Alberto Massi in October in Cordoba, Argentina. These were the last losses Carlos would ever suffer in a career that would include over 100 professional fights stretched over 13 years until his retirement in 1977.

Carlos would avenge all of his defeats in rematches and surprised everyone by winning the Argentine middleweight championship from Jorge Fernandez in September of 1966. Carlos and Amilcar Brusa formed a partnership with promoter Tito

Lectoure, and Carlos became a regular, fighting at the famed Luna Park arena in Buenos Aires.

In 1967, Carlos defeated Fernandez again for the South American middleweight title. Carlos remained undefeated in 1968 in 8 fights, and gained his first top 10 ranking in the middleweight division.

In January of 1969, Carlos knocked out Ruben Orrico in a South American middleweight title defense, and then decisioned world ranked middleweight contender Tom Bethea in August. In October, Carlos made the 2nd successful defense of his South American middleweight title when he knocked out Manuel Severino in 6 rounds.

Carlos won his first 6 matches in 1970 with only veteran middleweight Eddie Pace going the 10-round distance. Carlos had slowly crept up to the number one contender position for Nino Benvenuti's middleweight title. The title match was made with Benvenuti for November 7th in Rome, Italy. Benvenuti was a huge favorite in the fight because Carlos had never fought outside of South America and was largely unknown to the world wide boxing public.

When the fighters stepped into the ring, it was seen that Carlos, at nearly 6 feet in height, was actually taller than the 5-11-inch Benvenuti. Benvenuti may have been the favorite in the fight, but it was Carlos who came out aggressively and took the fight to Benvenuti. It appeared that Benvenuti could not gain his rhythm in the fight as Carlos muscled him around the ring and landed the harder punches.

After 10 rounds, Benvenuti was way behind in the scoring and he became desperate. Benvenuti started trying to slug with Carlos and he paid the price in the 12th round when Carlos drove him into a corner and measured him with a perfect right cross to the chin. Benvenuti dropped down heavily to the canvas. Benvenuti actually beat the referee's 10-count but when he got up, he wobbled into the ropes, and the referee stopped the fight. Everyone in the arena was shocked at the outcome of the fight with the exception of Monzon, Brusa, and Lectoure. Many boxing fans in Argentina were also shocked at the ending of the fight. It was obvious the way Carlos casually strolled to a neutral corner after the knockdown that he did not seemed surprised he could win the fight.

Benvenuti claimed in the Italian press that he just had an off night and that he wanted a rematch with Carlos as soon as possible. Carlos after basking in the limelight as world champion in Argentina, finally signed to defend his title against Benvenuti in May of 1971, in Monte Carlo.

Carlos proved that his title victory was no fluke, as he clearly manhandled Benvenuti in the rematch before the challenger's corner threw the white towel of surrender into the ring in the 3rd round. Even though Benvenuti kicked the towel out of the ring and protested the stoppage, it was clear to everyone at ringside that the champion was just too strong for him after he had been dropped and severely battered around the ring.

In September, Carlos defended the title against former Welterweight and Middleweight Champion Emile Griffith. Griffith had been a great fighter, but it was felt that he was a little bit past his prime. Griffith kept the fight close for the first 10 rounds, but Carlos youth and power started to take effect in the 11th round. Carlos eventually pounded Griffith into a 14th round technical knockout loss.

Carlos returned to Rome in March of 1972 to defend his title against American veteran Denny Moyer. Moyer had been fighting since the 1950s and he was the first world junior middleweight champion in 1962. The veteran Moyer had been on a middleweight winning streak to gain the title fight and he gave Carlos more than he expected in the fight. In a competitive fight the referee appeared to stop the fight way too soon in the 5th round after Moyer had been staggered by Carlos. The Italian crowd threw fruit into the ring to protest the Argentine referee's premature stoppage of the fight.

In June, Carlos traveled to Paris to defend against French fan favorite Jean Claude Bouttier. Carlos was cool and methodical in the ring as he hammered the game Frenchman into a 13th round technical knockout victory. Carlos was an intelligent fighter who could adjust to an opponent's style of fighting and he had a great sense of pace. In both the Griffith and Bouttier fights, he came on strong after the 10th round to stop his opponents.

In August, Carlos traveled to Copenhagen to take on Danish fighter Tom Bogs. Bogs had done well against European opponents but against Carlos he made the mistake of inflicting a cut on the champions face. Carlos became enraged and immediately stopped Bogs in the 5th round of the scheduled 15-round fight.

In November, Carlos returned to Buenos Aires to defend against top ranked Bennis Briscoe from Philadelphia. Carlos had previously fought to a draw with Briscoe in 1967 when he was an upcoming challenger to the title. In this title fight, Carlos was ahead on points when Briscoe rocked him with a left hook to the head in the 9th round. Carlos was momentarily stunned and grabbed onto the ropes for support. Carlos eventually cleared his head and boxed his way to a unanimous decision win over the tough Philadelphia fighter.

For his 4 successful title defenses in 1972, the Boxing Illustrated magazine voted Carlos their fighter of the year. Even though he was gaining worldwide fame, Carlos was still an unknown product in the United States. He would not fight in the United States until 1975.

Carlos returned to the ring in the spring of 1973 and knocked out Roy Dale in a non-title fight in Rome, Italy. In June, Carlos defended his title against Emile Griffith in a rematch in Monte Carlo. Griffith used all his ring experience to make the fight close again, but Carlos pulled the fight out in the last few rounds when Griffith faded badly.

Carlos took on Jean Claude Bouttier in another rematch in Paris in September. Bouttier put up a better fight against Carlos in the rematch and held the champion close for the first ten rounds. Carlos used his power to drop Bouttier in the late rounds and win another unanimous decision over the French fighter.

Carlos defended his belt against Welterweight Champion Jose Napoles in February of 1974, in Paris. Many ringside observers felt that Napoles had a chance to win the fight since Carlos did not look exceptionally well in winning his rematches with Griffith and Bouttier in 1973. Napoles nickname was "mantequilla" which means butter in Spanish as his ring style was described as smooth as butter.

Carlos was the much bigger man in the ring and he used his size and reach to good advantage. At the end of 6 rounds, Napoles' face was a mass of cuts and he was unable to come out for the 7th round. Carlos proved that he was far from finished as a super star of boxing, and he was starting to get the credit he deserved in the ring.

Carlos hinted at retirement after the Napoles fight and the World Boxing Council was quick to set up a match between Rodrigo Valdes and Bennie Briscoe for their version of the middleweight title. Valdes stopped Briscoe in May to get the World Boxing Council recognition as champion, but to the rest of the world Carlos was the World Boxing Association and, more importantly, the lineal middleweight champion of the world.

In October, Carlos defended his title against glass chinned Australian contender Tony Mundine in Buenos Aires. Mundine was able to dodge most of Carlos' right-hand bombs until the 7th round when he suddenly collapsed under the champion's pressure.

In June of 1975, Carlos traveled to Madison Square Garden in New York to take on number one contender Tony Licata from New Orleans. Licata was a slick boxer who had only lost one time in around 50 professional fights. Licata boxed smartly in the early rounds as Carlos appeared rather rusty and slow. Carlos picked up the pace around the 5th round and began battering Licata around the ring with his deadly right hands to the head and body. Carlos hurt and dropped Licata before the referee stopped the fight in the 10th round to save Licata from further punishment. The sports writers did not seem too impressed by Carlos performance, and one sportswriter described his style as "smooth as a cigar store Indian". Carlos ring style may not have been as flashy as Sugar Ray Robinson or Sugar Ray Leonard, but all he ever did was win all the time no matter who the opponent was.

In December of 1975, Carlos returned to Paris, France to defend against power punching Frenchman Gratien Tonna. Tonna was a muscular Frenchman who had done well against Europrean competiton but had quit in a title fight against Rodrigo Valdes in 1974 claiming a foul blow.

Carlos was ahead in the fight when he caught Tonna a blow to the side of his head. Tonna dropped to the canvas claiming a foul as he had done in the Valdes fight. The referee did not buy Tonna's act and counted him out. Apparently Tonna was trying to duplicate the feats of ex-French middleweight champion Marcel Thil who won at least 2 title fights by claiming fouls in the 1930s.

Carlos wished to unify his middleweight title before he retired. A match was made with Carlos fighting the World Boxing Council champion Rodrigo Valdes in June of 1976, in Monte Carlo

A week before the scheduled fight Valdes brother was killed in a barroom altercation in Colombia. Valdes was unable to postpone the fight, and the match went on as scheduled. The match was close and Valdes was starting to come on until Carlos dropped him in the

14th round and swept the last 2 rounds to take a close decision. Due to the circumstances of his brother's death, Valdes requested a rematch and Carlos gave it to him. The rematch was set for July of 1977, in Monte Carlo again.

In the rematch, Valdes started off fast, and dropped Carlos in the 2nd round with an overhand right to the jaw. Carlos got up and boxed his way out of trouble. Carlos showed his ring intelligence by side stepping Valdes' rushes and hitting him with lead right hands to the head. Carlos stormed into the lead in the middle rounds, and by the end of the fight Valdes face was cut and swollen. Carlos won another unanimous decision and finally retired from the ring in August.

Carlos was able to control his emotions inside of the ring, but outside of it was another story. During his boxing career Carlos had been shot by his first wife during a domestic dispute, and while still married he was carrying on an affair with Argentine actress Susanna Giminez. Carlos was also known for punching reporters and anyone else who aggravated him outside of the ring.

After his retirement Carlos married his second wife, Alicia Muniz, a pretty Argentine blond that he had met at an Argentine airport. Carlos and Muniz had a volatile relationship and in 1988 while on vacation together in Mar de Plata, Argentina they both fell to the ground from a hotel balcony after a domestic dispute. It was later proven that Carlos had choked Muniz into unconsciousness before her fall to the ground. Carlos was arrested for murder and went on trial. The trial drew nationwide attention similar to the O.J. Simpson trial in the 1990s in the United States.

Ultimately Carlos was found guilty and sentenced to 11 years in prison. Carlos claimed that it was his bad temper that he was unable to control that was responsible for all of his problems in life. Carlos went to prison in 1989 and, while on a prison release program, he died in a car accident returning to the prison in 1995. Carlos was

52 years of age at the time of his death. Carlos remained a hero to the sporting public in Argentina and today he is regarded by many as the greatest middleweight champion in history.

His ring style was not of flashy elegance, but more of a cool efficient style of fighting. He had a stiff left jab and a powerful right cross. He had split second timing in the ring and had a habit of leaning away from punches at the last second. He paced himself well and was coming on strong at the end of most of his fights. He was never stopped in a fight, and rarely cut.

Carlos ring record was 87 wins, 3 losses, and 9 draws. He won 59 fights by knockout. He was inducted in the International Boxing Hall of Fame in 1990.

Vito Antuofermo

Photograph from BoxRec

Vito Antuofermo

Vito Garbriello Antuofermo was born in the Puglia province of Italy on February 9, 1953. Vito came to the United States as a teenager and settled with his family in Brooklyn, New York.

Vito started training at the Police Athletic League in Brooklyn after he was picked up by the police for street fighting. As an amateur Vito won the 147-pound Golden Gloves title in 1970. Vito turned professional and obtained the services of local businessman Tony Carione as his manager.

Vito remained undefeated during his first 18 fights until he was stopped by Harold Weston in 5 rounds in July of 1973 on cuts. The tender skin around Vito's eyes would be an issue for him throughout his whole professional career.

After the Weston bout, Vito went on another winning streak that saw him beat former Welterweight and Middleweight Champion Emile Griffith, and former Junior Middleweight Champion Denny Moyer in 1974.

Vito continued his winning streak into 1975 when he won a close decision in a nationally televised fight with Vinnie Curto in August. Curto was a slick boxer but Vito's aggressiveness and strong finish was the difference in the fight.

In January of 1976, Vito dropped down to the 154-pound super welterweight limit to win the European super welterweight title over German Eckhard Dagge in Berlin, Germany. Vito handled the weight loss well and did not appear to lose any strength as he outfought Dagge to win a unanimous decision.

In March, Vito traveled to Milan, Italy to defend his title against Frenchman Jean-Claude Warusfel. Vito handed Warusfel a boxing lesson and then stopped him in the 14th round of the European title fight.

In June, Vito took on young German Frank Wissenbach in an 8-round non-title European fight in Berlin. Vito had trouble with the German's southpaw stance and lost a point on a foul to lose a close decision.

In October, Vito defended his European title against Britain's Maurice Hope in Rome, Italy. Vito started off well, but Hope caught up to him in the later rounds and stopped him in the 15th and last round of the title fight. Vito had problems making the super welterweight limit and returned to the middleweight division after the Hope fight.

In 1977, Vito won all 3 of his fights, including a knockout over savage punching Eugene (Cyclone) Hart of Philadelphia. In February of 1978, Vito returned to New York to take on Philadelphia slugger Bennie Briscoe. Briscoe had been the number one contender for the middleweight title for a number of years during the decade. Vito out fought and outhustled Briscoe to take a unanimous decision over the tough Philadelphia fighter. Vito finished out the year winning decisions over Willie Warren, Willie Classen, and Mike Hallacy to become the number one contender for Argentine Hugo Corro's middleweight title.

The title fight with Corro was set for April of 1979, but Corro pulled out of the fight claiming an injury. The title fight was finally set for June in Monte Carlo. The undercard featured Marvin Hagler taking on Argentine Norberto Cabrera.

Hagler stopped Cabrera in the 8th round of their preliminary match. In the main event title fight Vito got off to a slow start as Corro boxed well and piled up points. Vito had a point taken away by the referee during one of the middle rounds, and, after the end of 10 rounds, it appeared Vito was going to lose a decision. Vito began the 11th round using relentless aggression to drive Corro to the ropes in a defensive posture. Vito swept the last 5 rounds with his aggression to win a split decision and take the crown from the defensive minded Corro. Commentator Howard Cosell was telling the television audience that Corro was way ahead in the fight, when someone had to tell him that Vito had closed the gap during the late rounds. Cosell then correctly told the audience that the fight was now very close.

Everyone predicted a short title reign for Vito as his next scheduled opponent was going to be Marvin Hagler. The Hagler fight was set for November in Las Vegas, Nevada. Hagler was made the favorite in the fight by the oddsmakers, but they had no way of measuring Vito's heart.

Hagler started off fast in the fight, raking Vito's head and body with combinations and opening up cuts on his face. Vito's corner did an excellent job patching his cuts and allowing him to be competitive in the fight. Vito amazingly started to come on in the middle rounds and was actually backing Hagler up with his aggression. Both fighters took turns staggering each other during the last few rounds and the audience awaited the decision. The judges called the fight a draw, and Vito was allowed to keep his title. Most of the ringside press scored the fight for Hagler, but it was a close fight, and a rematch was in order.

Before a rematch could be made, the World Boxing Council mandated a defense against their number one contender, England's Alan Minter. Vito's match with Minter was scheduled for March of 1980, in Las Vegas. British promotor Mickey Duff showed up for the fight with a British entourage which included judge Roland Dakin.

Vito started off the fight in his usual slow fashion against the British southpaw who boxed well in the early going. Vito, as usual, started to come on strong in the middle rounds. It was apparent during the fight that referee Carlos Padilla was breaking the fighters up quickly, not allowing Vito to do much infighting. The fight was made close when Vito scored a knockdown in the 14th round and the two fighters battled on even terms in the last round. Both fighters were known to be "bleeders" but neither fighter suffered any serious cuts during the fight. Minter was awarded a split decision victory, which included the British judge awarding him 13 rounds in the close fight. The Associated Press scored the fight for Vito by a slight margin.

Due to the closeness of the fight and the British judges unusual scoring, a rematch was ordered between the two fighters. The rematch was set for June in London, England.

Vito was stopped in the 8th round of the rematch when his corner was unable to stop the bleeding from cuts on his face. Vito was cut all most immediately during the match and he never was really in the fight before it was stopped.

Vito fought for the title one more time in 1981 when he took on Marvin Hagler in Boston. Vito suffered a severe cut in this fight due to a head butt and the fight was stopped in the 5th round due to cuts. Hagler managed to drop Vito once before the fight was stopped.

Vito attempted a short comeback in 1984 and won a couple of fights before he was stopped by future Super Welterweight Champion Matthew Hilton in Montreal, Canada in October of 1985, and retired for good

In retirement, Vito got involved in the field of acting and actually had a small part in one of the Godfather movies. Vito also acted in a few plays in New York and today owns a prosperous landscaping company in Long Island, New York.

Vito's final ring record was 50 wins, 7 losses, and 2 draws. He won 21 fights by knockout. Vito was known as an aggressive fighter who had a lot of heart and stamina but, unfortunately, was susceptible to cuts. He was inducted into the World Boxing Hall of Fame in 1994.

Bennie Briscoe

Photograph from BoxRec

Bennie Briscoe

'Bad" Bennie Briscoe was born on February 8, 1943, in Augusta, Georgia, the eldest of 9 children. At the age of 16 he moved to Philadelphia to live with an aunt and uncle.

Bennie began training alongside Joe Frazier in Philadelphia and began a career in amateur boxing. Bennie reportedly compiled an amateur record of 70 wins and just 3 losses. He won the Middle Atlantic AAU amateur welterweight title three times.

Bennie turned professional as a welterweight on October 9, 1962, in Philadelphia with a 4-round decision over Sam Samuel. Bennie won his first 15 fights and scored 10 knockouts when he took on veteran Percy Manning in June of 1964. Manning took a 10-round decision and exposed some of his flaws such as being somewhat mechanical in the ring and slow afoot.

Bennie scored a couple of quick knockouts after the Manning loss, followed by losses to Tito Marshall, and Stanley "Kitten" Hayward before the end of 1965. In 1966, Bennie fought 3 times and capped off the year with a 1st round knockout of the talented George Benton. Bennie, now a middleweight, was gaining a reputation as an all action, aggressive, body punching fighter who could beat anyone on a good night and then turn around and lose a decision the next night to an average fighter. He had an aggressive crowd-pleasing style of boxing which brought the fans out in droves in Philadelphia.

Continuing with his problem of fighting slick moving boxers, Bennie lost a decision to crafty former Welterweight Champion Luis Rodriguez in March of 1967, and then flew to Buenos Aires, Argentina to do battle with future Middleweight Champion Carlos Monzon in May. Bennie was given a draw in his fight with Monzon, which means that if the fight was probably held anywhere else but in Argentina, he would have probably received the decision.

Bennie returned to Philadelphia and scored several knockouts before he was again decisioned by Luis Rodriguez in December of 1967. Bennie was heavy handed and could knock out anyone who stood in front of him and decided to slug, but he still remained inconsistent in the ring at this point of his career.

Bennie scored a couple of big wins in August of 1968 when he knocked out Gene (Honeybear) Bryant in 8 rounds, and won a decision over Jose Gonzalez in 10 rounds. Bennie had an even better year in 1969 as he stopped Vicente Rondon in January, Percy Manning in May, and Tito Marshall in September.

In 1970, Bennie won all 3 of his fights by knockout. He defeated Joe Shaw in May, Eddie Owens in September, and Harold Richardson in November. In 1971, Bennie knocked out Tom Bethea, Carlos Marks, and Juarez de Lima, to crack the top ten ratings in the middleweight division.

After a couple of quick knockout wins, Bennie took a tune up fight in March with unknown Luis Vinales before a proposed title fight with champion Carlos Monzon later in the year. Vinales was a huge underdog and he shocked Bennie by taking a 10-round decision in Philadelphia. In October, Bennie got a rematch with Vinales and stopped him in the 7th round to secure his title fight with Monzon in November in Buenos Aires.

Carlos was aware of Bennie's power and boxed smartly during the first 8 rounds of the fight. In the 9th round Bennie caught

Carlos with a perfect left hook to the jaw, which made Monzon wobble briefly and grab a top ring rope for support. Bennie appeared surprised and did not go immediately after Monzon, thus losing his chance for a knockout. Monzon lasted out the round and then proceeded to outbox Bennie for the remainder of the fight to win a unanimous decision. Monzon would later state after his career was over that Bennie was one of the toughest and hardest hitting opponents that he had ever faced in the ring.

Bennie scored 5 knockout wins in 1973, but lost a 12-round decision to Colombian Rodrigo Valdes in Noumea in September. In February of 1974, Bennie was matched with number one middleweight contender Tony Mundine in Paris, France. Mundine was an Australian who had defeated Emile Griffith and was being primed for a title shot at the middleweight championship.

Mundine, who was known as a knockout artist, came out strong at the first bell and rocked Bennie during the first two rounds. Bennie started to turn the fight around in the 3rd round, and finally stopped the weak chinned Australian in the 5th round.

The World Boxing Council had stripped Carlos Monzon as world champion for varied invalid reasons and set up a fight between Bennie and Rodrigo Valdes for the vacant title. The title fight was set for May in Monte Carlo. Valdes out boxed Bennie during the first 5 rounds, but then suffered a facial laceration. Bennie was starting to take command of the fight until he ran into a straight right hand from Valdes that knocked him down on the seat of his pants. Bennie got up dazed before the 10-count, but the referee stopped the fight and declared Valdes the winner by technical knockout. This was the only time Bennie was ever stopped in his professional career.

After having blown his second title shot, Bennie returned to Philadelphia and looked terrible as he was completely out boxed by an aging Emile Griffith in October. In 1975, Bennie quietly started working on an unbeaten streak which would eventually lead him to a 3rd try at the middleweight title.

In 1975, Bennie won decisions over Stanley (Kitten) Hayward and Eddie Gregory. In 1976, he knocked out Eugene (Cyclone) Hart in 1 round and boxed to a draw with Emile Griffith. In March of 1977, Bennie knocked out Jean Mateo in Paris, France and Sammy Barr in July in Philadelphia.

In August of 1977, Carlos Monzon announced his retirement from the ring and a fight for the vacant world title was set up between Bennie and old rival Rodrigo Valdes. Bennie had been unbeaten since 1974, and this would be his third and last try at the world title.

The title fight was held in Campione d'Italia in November. Both Bennie and Valdes were probably a little bit past their prime for this battle and it was a competitive fight. Rodrigo boxed well, and was a little too quick for Bennie as he walked away with the decision and the world title. Bennie complained about the decision, but most ringsiders felt that Valdes had done enough to win the fight

Bennie continued fighting and lost decisions in 1978 to future World Middleweight Champions Vito Antuofermo and Marvin Hagler. He would continue on in the ring with mixed success until his final retirement in 1982.

Bennie was described as the 'quintessential' Philadelphia fighter with his shear aggression in the ring, and nobody could draw a crowd of fight fans to a fight in Philadelphia like him. He was a top contender for the middleweight title for most of the decade in the 1970s but, unfortunately, he always seemed to fall just short in his attempts to win the title. After retirement from the ring, Bennie worked in the sanitation department for the City of Philadelphia for over 20 years.

Bennie's final ring record was 66 wins, 24 losses, and 5 draws. He won 53 fights by knockout. Bennie was inducted into the World Boxing Hall of Fame in 2010. Bennie also passed away in 2010 at the age of 67 after a short illness.

Jose Napoles

Photograph from BoxRec

Chapter 4   Top Welterweights of the Decade

Jose Napoles

Jose "Mantequilla" Napoles was born in Santiago de Cuba, Cuba on April 13, 1940. His amateur record is an unverified 113-1 or 114-1 in Cuba. Jose turned professional on August 2, 1958, by knocking out Julio Rojas in 1 round in Havana. Jose won his first 7 professional fight and then lost to Hilton Smith in August of 1959, in his first 10-round fight.

Jose won 6 of 7 fights in 1960 and won his first 3 fights by knockout in 1961 before Fidel Castro outlawed professional boxing in Cuba. Jose moved his base of operations to Mexico in 1962 and knocked out Enrique Camarena in 2 rounds in July in Mexico City. Jose's aggressive style of pin point counterpunching and his smooth style of fighting earned him the nickname of "Mantequilla", which means butter in Spanish.

Jose won all 4 of his fights in 1962 in Mexico, and by years end he was ranked in the top ten in the world in the junior welterweight division. Jose got off to a slow start in 1963 losing 2 of his first 4 fights but he ended the year by winning his last 5 fights by knockout. His knockout victims included Raul Soriano and L.C. Morgan

In 1964, Jose soared to the top of the junior welterweight rankings with knockouts of Alfredo Urbina in April in Mexico City, and top contender Carlos Hernandez of Venezuela in Caracas in

June. The knockout of Hernandez was considered an upset and Jose solidified his number one ranking by knocking out Urbina in a rematch in Mexico City in November.

Jose knocked out L.C. Morgan in a rematch in Mexico City in February of 1965, and won a decision over former Junior Welterweight Champion Eddie Perkins in August in Juarez, Mexico. Jose was calling for a title match with new Junior Welterweight Champion Carlos Hernandez, but apparently Hernandez had other plans while remembering the result of his first match with Jose.

Jose won 5 fights by knockout in 1966 but was stopped by L.C. Morgan on cuts in August and temporarily lost his number one contender position. In 1967, Jose moved up to the welterweight division and won all 4 fights by knockout, including a 2-round stoppage of L.C. Morgan in a July rematch in Tijuana, Mexico.

Jose won all 7 fights in 1968, including wins over top contenders Peter Cobblah, Eddie Pace, and Lennox Beckles. By years end Jose was elevated to the number one contender position for Curtis Cokes' welterweight title.

Jose knocked out Fate Davis in 7 rounds in February, and then challenged Cokes for the welterweight title in Los Angeles, California in April of 1969. Cokes fought gamely in defense of his title but Jose fought a perfect fight and, at the end of 13 rounds, Coke's eyes were swollen shut by Jose's pin point counterpunching. Cokes could not continue the battle and Jose was the new welterweight champion of the world. Mexican fans who had made the trip from Mexico to see the fight went wild when Jose was announced as the new champion. Cokes asked for a rematch and it would take place in June in Mexico City.

The result was the same in the rematch, except this time it took Jose only 10 rounds to stop Cokes. The two physical beatings that Jose gave Cokes would finish him as a top contender in boxing.

Ex-welterweight and middleweight champion Emile Griffith dropped back down to the welterweight limit to challenge Jose for his title in October in Los Angeles. A national television audience would get to see just how good Jose really was.

The fight was not even close as Jose dominated Griffith throughout the whole fight to take an easy 15-round decision. The boxing public was surprised at the ease in which Jose handled the former champion in the ring. At this point the worldwide audience finally realized what a well-schooled and brilliant fighter Jose really was.

In February of 1970, top contender Ernie (Indian Red) Lopez challenged Jose for the title in Los Angeles. Lopez had quite a following in the Los Angeles area and the fight drew a large crowd. Lopez was made to order for Jose's style of fighting. Lopez liked to lead with his right hand, which made him a perfect target for Jose's counter punches. Lopez put up a brave battle but Jose finally caught up to him and stopped him in the 15th and final round.

In December, Jose traveled to Syracuse, New York to take on local favorite Billy Backus. Backus was a huge underdog and one of his punches cut Jose severely during an early exchange and the fight was stopped and awarded to Backus. Jose claimed the cut was caused by a butt, but the result remained unchanged as a 4th round technical knockout for Backus. From this point on, cuts would remain a problem for Jose in the ring.

Jose returned to the ring in March of 1971 and stopped former top contender Manuel Gonzalez in 6 rounds in Mexico City. Jose then signed to challenge Backus for the title in a rematch set for June in Los Angeles. Jose received a small cut from Backus again in the first round. This time the cut was minor, and Jose really went to work on Backus with vicious combinations that closed one of his eyes and puffed the other eye up. By the 8th round, Backus was a mess with cuts all over his face and the referee wisely stopped the fight to save him from further punishment.

In December of 1971, Jose defended his title against Hedgemon Lewis in Los Angeles. Lewis was a slick boxer who had great foot movement and fast hands. Lewis remained competitive in the fight, but Jose's power was the difference and he won a close decision to retain his title.

Jose defended his title in 1972 by traveling to London to stop Ralph Charles in 7 rounds in March, and knock out old foe, Adolph Pruitt, in 3 rounds in June in Monterey, Mexico. In February of 1973, Jose gave Ernie (Indian Red) Lopez a rematch in Los Angeles. Jose was cut severely early in the fight and he had to come from behind to stop Lopez with an uppercut which ripped open a cut across his eye causing Lopez to sink to the canvas in great pain for the 10-count in the 7th round.

In June, Jose traveled to Grenoble to take an easy 15-round decision over Frenchman Roger Menetrey. In September, Jose defended his title in Toronto against local Canadian challenger Clyde Gray. Gray fought on even terms with Jose before he was over powered in the late rounds and lost a close decision to the champion. Next up for Jose was a fight for Carlos Monzon's middleweight title in February in Paris, France.

This was the super fight that the boxing public was waiting for. The tall, rugged middleweight champion against the smooth punching welterweight champion. Monzon did not look particularly good in beating Emile Griffith and Jean Claude Bouttier in rematches in 1973, and some boxing experts thought Jose had a good chance to take the middleweight title.

Jose opened the fight aggressively coming at Monzon and taking the first two rounds on the scorecards. Monzon kept snapping out his jab and began catching Jose coming inside with quick right hands. Jose started to slow down in the fourth round, and he was severely hurt and cut in the 5th round. Monzon battered Jose all over the ring in the 6th round and his corner would not let him come out for the 7th round. Napoles claimed that he caught a thumb in his eye but it looked more like a case of a good big man, beating a good little man.

Jose returned to the ring to make 2 successful title defenses in 1974. Jose stopped Hedgemon Lewis in 9 rounds in August, and stopped Argentine Horacio Saldano in 3 rounds in December. Both title defenses took place in Mexico City.

In March of 1975, Jose defended his title against Armando Muniz in Acapulco. Jose received severe cuts during the fight and it was stopped in the 12th round. The officials ruled that the cuts were due to butts and Napoles was given a 12-round technical decision. It appeared that the cuts were due more to punches so Muniz was given a rematch in Mexico City in July. Jose decked Muniz in the rematch and won a convincing 15-round unanimous decision.

In December, Jose defended his title against top British contender John H. Stracey in Mexico City. Jose dropped Stracey in the first round, but Stracey boxed well after the knockdown and opened up severe cuts on Jose's face that caused the fight to be stopped in the 6th round. Jose wisely chose to retire after his title loss to Stracey.

Jose's final ring record was 81 wins, and 7 losses. He won 54 fights by knockout. Jose will go down in boxing history as one of the greatest welterweight champions of all time and he is regarded as a ring legend in his adopted country of Mexico. He was inducted into the International Boxing Hall of Fame in 1990. Jose currently lives with his family in Chihuahua, Mexico.

Carlos Palomino

Photograph from BoxRec

Carlos Palomino

Carlos Palomino was born on August 10, 1949, in San Luis Potosi, Mexico. Carlos moved with his family to the Los Angeles, California area when he was 10 years old. As an amateur boxer he was an all US Army Champion in 1971 and 1972. Carlos also won the National AAU light welterweight title defeating Olympian Sugar Ray Seales.

After being discharged from the Army, Carlos started community college and turned to professional boxing in September of 1972 with a 4-round decision over Javier Martinez. Carlos obtained the services of famed Los Angeles manager and trainer Jackie McCoy and was undefeated in his first 11 professional fights. His first loss occurred in August of 1974 when he lost a split decision to welterweight contender Andy (Hawk) Price.

In February of 1975, Carlos drew with rated contender Zovek Barajas, and then knocked him out in the rematch in 9 rounds in March in Los Angeles. McCoy had developed Carlo's body punching skills and kept him in top shape at all times. In November, Carlos fought to a draw with top welterweight contender Hedgemon Lewis. After two quick wins at the Olympic auditorium in Los Angeles, McCoy was able to get Carlos a title shot at World Boxing Council Welterweight Champion John H. Stracey in June in London.

Carlos was unknown outside of Los Angeles, and Stracey was a big favorite with the British fans in London. Stracey had won the title from the legendary Jose Napoles in December of 1974, and

75

had looked unbeatable when he knockout out contender Hedgemon Lewis in 10 rounds in London in March. It could be said that the British fans just saw Carlos as a mere tune up fight for their local hero.

McCoy had a working relationship with Mickey Duff and some of the British promoters, but they did not really realize how tough an opponent they had chosen for a title defense for Stracey. The locals soon found out as Carlos took all that Stracey could throw at him and then started opening up with his customary withering body attack. By the 10th round, Carlos had caught up to Stracey in the scoring and he was dishing out a severe body beating. By the 12th round, Stracey was screaming out in pain from the body blows and he could not continue. The British fans were stunned as they had not expected the American to be such a devastating body puncher.

Carlos and McCoy flew back to California to await the challenge from cross town rival Armando (the man) Muniz. The fight with Muniz would pit two college graduates in the same ring, fighting for a world title. The Palomino vs. Muniz match was a promoter's dream in the Los Angeles area as the huge Hispanic population was divided on their loyalties to their own local fighters.

The fight took place in January of 1977, and Muniz came out aggressively and dropped Carlos in the early going of fight. After 10 rounds, Muniz was still ahead in the scoring, but Carlos was starting to come on down the home stretch with his customary late rounds body attack. Muniz had not paced himself well and started to wilt. By the end of 14 rounds the fight was virtually even on the scorecards. Carlos was the fresher fighter going into the last round, and he dropped Muniz in the 15th round. The referee stopped the contest with about 30 seconds to go as Muniz was unable to continue. Carlos had just won a come from behind dramatic fight by a 15th round technical knockout. Muniz was livid that the fight was stopped, however he would have lost the fight on points had he made it to the final bell anyway.

In June, Carlos was back in London to defend against David (Boy) Green. Green was an aggressive fighter and had more of an American style of boxing. Green's style of fighting was made to order for Carlos as he gave Green a beating and knocked him cold in the 11th round. By this time the British had probably seen enough of Carlos and his manager Jackie McCoy.

In September, Carlos returned to Los Angeles to defend against fringe contender Everaldo Costa Azevedo. Azevedo proved to be more of a runner then a fighter and he ran for 15 rounds just to last the limit against Carlos. Azevedo succeeded in lasting the limit but Carlos won an easy decision in a lackluster fight.

In December, Carlos took on another fringe contender in Mexico's Jose Palacio's in Los Angeles. At least Palacios came to fight and gave it his all before Carlos overpowered him in the 13th round for a technical knockout victory over the game Mexican.

In February of 1978, Carlos defended against Ryu Sorimachi in Las Vegas. Carlos overpowered the hapless Japanese fighter in the 7th round, and then defended again the following month in Las Vegas against another fringe contender in Mimoun Mohatar. Carlos stopped Mohatar in the 9th round of the non-competitive fight. It was obvious that McCoy was a shrewd manager in his careful selection of Carlos opponent's, but in May a rematch was made with Armando Muniz with the title on the line

Carlos did not need a late round knockout to win the fight in the rematch as he took a convincing 15-round decision over Muniz. It appeared that Muniz did not do well in rematches as he also failed against Jose Napoles in a rematch after his first controversial loss to him in Acapulco.

Carlos was mandated by the World Boxing Council to defend against young Puerto Rican hotshot Wilfred Benitez in January of

1979. The fight took place in San Juan, Puerto Rico and was televised nationally in the United States.

Carlos got off to his customary slow start in the fight as Benitez proved to be an elusive target to hit in the early going. Carlos did come on a bit in the fight but Benitez always appeared to stay one step ahead of danger. Benitez received a well-deserved split decision win and Carlos was now an ex-champion. This would be the last title fight of Carlo's career.

In June of 1979, Carlos took on another legend in Panama's Roberto Duran on another nationally televised fight. If anything, Carlos proved that he had a chin in this fight as he took everything that Duran threw at him and fought back. Carlos lost a unanimous decision but he gained a lot of fans with his courageous effort. Carlos retired for the first time after this fight to begin an acting and television career.

After an 18-year absence from the ring, Carlos returned in 1997 to start a comeback. Carlos actually looked good as he won several comeback fights but he came up short against world ranked contender Wilfredo Rivera in a fight at the Olympic Auditorium in May of 1998, and retired for good.

Carlos will always be known for his incredible stamina, vicious body punching, and cast-iron chin. His final ring record was 31 wins, 4 losses, and 3 draws. He won 19 fights by knockout and was never stopped in any of his professional fights.

It is unfortunate that a title unification match was never made with the World Boxing Association Welterweight Champion Jose (Pipino) Cuevas of Mexico. The fight would have been a natural for Los Angeles but the fight was never made for political or promotional reasons. It is a shame because the fight fan was really the victim in this fight not being made. If I had to make a prediction, I feel that Carlos would have been able to take all of Cuevas early round bombs and then would have come back in the late rounds for a technical knockout victory.

Since retirement Carlos has served a term as chairman of the California State Athletic Commission and has done a lot of charity work. Carlos was inducted into the International Boxing Hall of Fame in 2004.

Pipino Cuevas

Photograph from BoxRec

Pipino Cuevas

Jose (Pipino) Cuevas was born on December 27, 1957, in Mexico City, Mexico. Pipino (which means Cucumber in Spanish) was his accepted ring name. Pipino turned professional at the age of 13 under the guidance of famed Mexican manager and trainer, Lupe Sanchez. Pipino lost his pro debut in November of 1971 by knockout and won only 7 out of his first 11 matches as he was fighting full grown men and had very raw boxing skills.

Under the guidance of Sanchez, Pipino won all 4 of his fights by knockout in 1974. In 1975 Pipino moved up in class and won the Mexican welterweight title by knocking out Jose Palacios in 10 rounds in September. In April of 1976, Pipino defended the national title by knocking out Rafael Piemonte in one round in Mexico City. Pipino gave up his national title to fight welterweight contender Andy Price in Los Angeles in June. Price proved to be to too ring wise and gave Pipino a boxing lesson to win a 10-round decision. World Boxing Association Welterweight Champion Angel Espada was looking for an easy title defense in July and Pipino was considered a far less dangerous opponent for the champion then the veteran Price. Espada defended his title against Pipino on July 17, in a bull ring in Mexicali, Mexico.

Pipino shocked Espada and the boxing world by knocking out the champion in the 2nd round of the title fight with a devastating left hook. Pipino was a world champion at the age of 18. His left hook was like a sickle and he was able to unleash tremendous power when he threw it. Pipino was definitely a one punch knockout artist.

In October, Lupe Sanchez took the young champion to Japan to defend against Japanese contender Shoji Tsujimoto in Tokyo. Pipino battered the game challenger senseless in 6 rounds of nonstop action. Pipino returned to the ring in March of 1977 to take on Argentine veteran Miguel Angel Campanino in Mexico City.

Campanino was the number one World Boxing Association contender for Pipino's title, and he was a legend in South America. Campanino had been a professional fighter for about 10 years, and he had over 80 wins to his credit with just 4 losses. Campanino was the favorite in the betting odds to take the title from the young and relatively inexperienced champion.

All Pipino had to do was touch an opponent with his left hook to end a fight and in the 2nd round the champion nailed Campanino flush with his hook and the fight was over. The Argentine press was shocked that their hero could be dismantled so quickly, but then again, Campanino had never been hit by any fighter that had the power that Pipino carried in his left hook.

Pipino returned to Los Angeles in August and destroyed Canadian veteran Clyde Gray in 2 rounds with the left hook. This was the same Clyde Gray who extended Jose Napoles 15 rounds in a recent welterweight title fight.

In November, Pipino defended against Angel Espada in a rematch in San Juan, Puerto Rico. Espada did better in the rematch as he extended the fight to 10 rounds, but he absorbed a frightful beating before the fight was stopped to save him from further punishment. Espada's face was swollen and misshaped after the fight and he had the appearance of a gargoyle.

In March of 1978, Pipino was back in Los Angeles defending his title against New York veteran Harold Weston. Weston hung in there with Pipino with his slick boxing skills, but he eventually suffered a broken jaw and the fight had to be stopped in the 9th round.

Pipino returned to Los Angeles in May and took on former Welterweight Champion Billy Backus. Backus could not get out of the way of Pipino's left hook and he suffered a broken orbital bone and damage to one eye in the first round of the fight. Pipino was not just knocking people out, he was breaking jaws and bones in opponents faces with the left hook.

In September, Pipino came to Sacramento, California to defend against the new number one World Boxing Association contender Pete Ranzany. Ranzany was the local fighter and the fight was held outdoors in Hughes Stadium. This writer was at the fight seated at ringside.

Pipino rushed out at the sound of the first bell, but Ranzany was making him miss most of his power punches. Ranzany kept a stiff jab in Pipino's face and would occasionally hit him with a straight right hand. Ranzany clearly out boxed Pipino in the first round, and actually made him look rather clumsy in the ring. Ranzany was very confident as the 2nd round started and made the mistake of trading punches with Pipino. While Ranzany was looking for the left hook, Pipino actually stunned him with a right hand and dropped him with the left hook. Ranzany got up but Pipino battered him across the ring and dropped him with another left hook. Ranzany got up again but the referee wisely stopped the fight as Ranzany did not look like he could continue the fight. This writer was simply amazed at the power in Pipino's left hook.

In January of 1979, Scott Clark challenged Pipino for the title in Los Angeles. Clark was an unknown and this fight should have never been made. Pipino battered Clark at will until the mismatch was stopped in the 2nd round.

In July, Pipino was challenged by top ten contender Randy Shields in Chicago, Illinois. Chicago had a large Hispanic population and the promotors hoped for a big gate for the fight. Shields fought a smart fight against Pipino as he avoided most of his power punches and would hit him with right hand leads before he could get set to punch. Shields also counterpunched well and Pipino won a very close 15-round decision to defend his title. This fight showed that Pipino could be out boxed, and that he was only human in the ring.

Pipino fought Angel Espada a third time in Los Angeles in December. Espada's aggressive style was made to order for Pipino as he gave Espada another systematic beating and stopped him in the 10th round. Thankfully this would be the last fight between these two fighters.

In April of 1980, Pipino defended against South African contender Harold Volbrecht in Houston, Texas. Volbrecht did well for the first 5 rounds, but in the 6th round he caught one of Pipino's power punches and the fight was stopped.

In August of 1980, Pipino traveled to Detroit, Michigan to take on top ranked Thomas (Hitman) Hearns. Hearns was a tall long armed puncher who was undefeated and fought out of the local very popular Kronk gym. As the fighters came to the center of the ring for the pre-fight instructions, the size difference was huge. Pipino at around 5-9 in height appeared to be close to a half foot shorter than Hearns and was at a substantial reach disadvantage also.

The bell rang for the first round and Hearns kept his long jab in Pipino's face when he was not clobbering him with straight right hands that wobbled him. Pipino swung his left hook at Hearns but he just simply could not reach the challenger. Pipino was hurt and dazed when the bell rang to end the first round.

Hearns came out for the second round looking for the knockout. He dropped Pipino with a straight right hand and when Pipino got up wobbling all over the ring, his corner threw the white towel in the ring to end the fight. The loss for Pipino was devastating as he was never really in the fight at any time. Pipino would never again fight for a title

In June of 1981, he flashed some of his old power as he knocked out European top welterweight Jorgen Hansen. The Hansen victory set up a super Latino showdown fight with the Panamanian legend Roberto Duran in January of 1983. Pipino started the fight aggressively and won the first two rounds, but Duran was able to roll with the punches and started to slow Pipino down with his own combinations to the head and body in the 3rd round. It was obvious that Duran took a punch much better the Pipino could and he dropped Pipino hard to the canvas in the 4th round. Pipino got up on unsteady legs and his corner again threw the white towel in the ring to end another of his fights.

Pipino had one good fight left in him when he took on number one World Boxing Association Venezuelan contender Mauricio Bravo in the old Olympic Auditorium in March of 1984. This writer attended this fight and saw Pipino come out aggressively in the first round and catch Bravo with his famed left hook. The fight was all over before Bravo could even get warmed up. It was the last of a typical Pipino Cuevas blowout fight against a top-rated contender.

Instead of getting another title shot, Pipino would go on to lose to Felipe Vaca in February of 1986, and retire after getting knocked out by Lupe Aquino in September of 1989. It was incredible how far Pipino went in the boxing game with the use of a powerful left hook. Pipino basically had no jab whatsoever and very poor footwork. He did have good stamina but his chin failed him in the latter part of his career. Between the years of 1976 to 1980 he was a pure destructible force in the welterweight division.

Pipino's final ring record was 35 wins and 15 losses. He won 31 fights by knockout. After winning the welterweight title he made 11 successful title defenses. Unfortunately, a title unification match with World Boxing Council champion Carlos Palomino never materialized. I would have picked Palomino to win that fight, but it would have been an exciting fight and a sure sell out with the large Hispanic population Los Angeles.

Today Pipino owns a string of butcher shops in Mexico City as well as a large security company. He was inducted into the International Boxing Hall of Fame in 2002.

Roberto Duran

Photograph from BoxRec

Chapter 5 Top Lightweights of the Decade

Roberto Duran

Roberto Duran Samaniego was born on June 16, 1951, in Chorillo, Panama. Chorillo was a violent ghetto located on the outskirts of Panama City. He shortened his ring name to Roberto Duran and turned professional under the guidance of manager Carlos Eleta in February of 1968, when he defeated Carlos Mendoza by decision in Colon, Panama.

Roberto had power in both fists and fought aggressively. He was nicknamed "Manos de Piedra" which means hands of stone in English. At 5 feet 7 inches in height he had no problem making the lightweight limit of 135 pounds.

After Roberto's win in his professional debut, he won the rest of his fights by knockout in 1968. Roberto continued his undefeated streak in 1969 by winning all 6 of his fights with 5 knockouts to his credit. Roberto cracked the top ten lightweight world rankings in 1970 when he won a unanimous decision from top ten contender Felipe Torres in March and then came back to stop Ernesto Marcel in 10 rounds in May.

Roberto won all 8 of his fights in 1971, including 7 knockout victories. In January of 1972, he won a unanimous decision from Angel Robinson Garcia to become the number one contender for Ken Buchanen's world lightweight title. In March, Roberto tuned up for his world title fight by knocking out Panchito Munoz in 1 round. In

June of 1972, Roberto challenged Ken Buchanen for the world lightweight title in New York's Madison Square Garden.

Ken Buchanen had won the lightweight title with a decision over Ismael Laguna in 1970, had successfully defended his title against Ruben Navarro, and Laguna in a rematch. He only had one questionable loss with over 40 victories. The slick boxing Scotsman was considered to be too slick and experienced for the relatively unknown Roberto.

Roberto took the fight to Buchanen with relentless pressure from the first round on. Buchanen could not seem to keep Roberto off of him and was way behind in the scoring when it appeared that Buchanen got hit low at or after the bell ending the 12th round. Buchanen could not come out of his corner for the 13th round and Roberto was crowned the new lightweight champion. It was a rather controversial ending to a fight that Roberto had dominated, and probably would have won no matter what happened at the final bell.

Roberto did not defend his title during the year, and he lost a 10-round non-title fight decision to Puerto Rican challenger Esteban DeJesus in November at Madison Square Garden. Roberto returned to Panama after the loss to DeJesus and defended his title against Jimmy Robertson instead of DeJesus in January of 1973. Robertson lacked the punch to keep Roberto off of him and he was stopped in the 5th round of a one-sided title defense. In June, Roberto defended his title against top Australian contender Hector Thompson. Roberto dismantled his opponent with vicious head and body combinations for an easy 8th round technical knockout. In September, Japanese contender Ishimatsu Suzuki came to Panama, but suffered the same fate as Thompson, as he finally succumbed to Roberto's relentless attack in the 10th round.

In March of 1974, Roberto finally gave Esteban DeJesus a shot at his title in a rematch held in Panama City. DeJesus got off to a fast start again, dropping Roberto in the first round. Roberto came roaring back and was relentless in his pursuit of the Puerto Rican challenger. DeJesus fought back with all of his artillery, but Roberto finally caught up to him in the 11th round to avenge the only loss in his career.

In December, Roberto knocked out hapless challenger Masataka Takayama in 1 round, and in March of 1975, Roberto gave challenger Ray Lampkin a systematic beating before finally stopping him in the 14th round. Roberto was vicious in the ring as he was always looking for the knockout and made comments to the press after the Lampkin fight that his goal was to destroy all of his opponents.

In December, Roberto stopped Mexican Leoncio Ortiz in the 15th round of a title fight, and boxing experts were wondering if Roberto was just allowing his opponents to last into the late rounds of title fights so that he could inflict as much punishment as possible on them.

In May of 1976, powder puff puncher Lou Bizarro took a terrible beating before Roberto caught up to him and stopped him in the 14th round. Roberto stopped Alvaro Rojas in 1 round of an easy title defense in Hollywood, Florida. In January of 1977, Roberto took on slick boxing top contender Vilomar Fernandez in Miami Beach, Florida. Fernandez was competitive in the fight, and Roberto had to work hard to finally stop Fernandez in the 13th round.

In September of 1977, Robert defended his title on national television against Puerto Rican contender Edwin Viruet in Philadelphia. Roberto had won a 10-round decision over Viruet in a non-title fight in 1975, but Roberto did not look good in that fight as he was unable to catch Viruet with any of his deadly combinations. Roberto won a unanimous decision in the title fight but he sustained a cut eye and was unable to finish Viruet before the final bell.

In January of 1978, Roberto fought a rubber match with Esteban DeJesus in Las Vegas, Nevada. Roberto won the rubber match by a 12th round knockout to win 2 of their 3 fights in their boxing trilogy, and unify the world lightweight title.

Roberto moved up to the welterweight division in 1979 and won a nationally television fight over former welterweight champion Carlos Palomino. Roberto dropped and dominated Palomino to win the unanimous decision.

In June of 1980, Roberto challenged Sugar Ray Leonard for the world welterweight championship in Montreal, Canada. Roberto was the underdog in the fight as Leonard had lifted the title from Wilfred Benitez in November of 1979 and was unbeaten as a professional. Leonard was considered the golden boy of boxing as he had also won an Olympic gold medal as an amateur.

To the surprise of many, Leonard chose not to box and moved around the ring. Roberto welcomed Leonard's change in strategy and outfought him to win a unanimous decision and the welterweight title. Duran as a two-division champion became a national hero in Panama after this victory.

Roberto gave Leonard a rematch for the title in November. Roberto was behind on points when he suddenly turned his back to Leonard and quit fighting, thus losing by an 8th round technical knockout. It appeared that Roberto had become frustrated during the fight as he was unable to catch up to Leonard before he suddenly just quit. Roberto made some comments after the fight that he quit because of some mysterious stomach ailment and this became known as the "no mas" fight. No mas meaning "no more" in English

In January of 1982, Roberto challenged Wilfred Benitez for the super welterweight championship. Benitez turned out to be too slick for Roberto and won a decision in a somewhat boring fight. It appeared that Roberto had lost a step in the ring and some ring scribes were calling for his retirement.

In January of 1983, he stopped former welterweight champion Pipino Cuevas in 4 rounds in Los Angeles in a big Latino super showdown between two Hispanic legends of the ring. In June of 1983, Roberto challenged Davey Moore for another shot at the super welterweight championship. Moore was undefeated and the favorite in the fight.

Roberto gave Moore a terrible beating dropping him and closing his eyes in winning a bloody 8th round technical victory to take the super welterweight championship. Roberto appeared to be ageless in taking his 3rd world title.

In November, Roberto challenged for his 4th world title when he took on champion Marvin Hagler for his middleweight title. Roberto made a valiant effort and the fight was even after 13 rounds. Hagler won the last 2 rounds on the scorecards to take a close unanimous decision.

In June of 1984, Roberto fought Thomas Hearn in an attempt to regain part of the world super welterweight title. Roberto could not get past Hearn's reach and was knocked flat on his face for the count in the 2nd round of the title fight.

In February of 1989, Roberto fought his last great fight. He challenged a much bigger and stronger Iran Barkley for his World Boxing Council middleweight championship. Barkley at 6 feet tall, had about a 5 inch height advantage over Roberto and he had knocked out Thomas Hearns for the middleweight title.

Roberto fought an inspired fight and even dropped Barkley to win a popular 12-round split decision to take the middleweight title. Roberto was now in the elite class of boxers who had won 4 world titles.

Roberto never defended his middleweight title and he lost a rubber match by decision to Sugar Ray Leonard in December of 1989. Roberto fought on for another 10 years and was stopped by William Joppy in 3 rounds in an attempt to regain the World Boxing Association middleweight title in August of 1998. Roberto would finally retire after losing to Hector Camacho by decision in July of 2001.

In a 33-year ring career, Roberto won 103 fights, lost 16, and won 70 fights by knockout. Roberto is a boxing legend and is still regarded as a hero in his home country of Panama. Many boxing analysts consider him to be the greatest lightweight champion in history. Roberto was inducted into the International Boxing Hall of Fame in 2007.

Esteban DeJesus

Photograph from Boxing Illustrated, November 1973

Esteban DeJesus

Esteban DeJesus was born on August 2, 1951, in Carolina, Puerto Rico. Nicknamed Vita, Esteban turned professional with a 3rd round knockout over El Tarita in February of 1969. Esteban won all 7 of his fights in 1969, with 6 wins coming by knockout.

Esteban continued to wipe out the local competition in Puerto Rico by winning all 10 of his fights in 1970, with 8 wins coming by knockout. In July of 1971, Esteban won the Puerto Rican lightweight title with a 12-round unanimous decision win over Josue Marquez. Esteban successfully defended his Puerto Rican title against Marquez in September with another unanimous decision win.

In October, Esteban traveled to Caracas, Venezuela to begin a 4-bout tour. In October, Esteban won a 10-round decision over ranked contender Leonel Hernandez, knocked out Frank Leroy in 7 rounds, and Milton Mendez in 5 rounds. In December, Esteban suffered his first loss when Antonio Gomez beat him by a 10-round unanimous decision

In 1972, Esteban returned to Puerto Rico and defeated lightweight contender Percy Hayles by unanimous decision in February, and defended his Puerto Rican lightweight title by knocking out Jose Marquez in 12 rounds in May. Esteban won a 10-round decision over veteran Doc McClendon in San Juan before traveling to New York's Madison Square Garden to take on world lightweight champion Roberto Duran in a non-title fight.

Esteban surprised everyone in the Garden by dropping Duran in the very first round. Esteban boxed smartly and avoided most of Duran's power punches to win a 10-round unanimous decision over the previously undefeated lightweight champion. DeJesus became the number one lightweight contender after this fight, but there would be no immediate title match against Duran.

In February of 1973, Esteban would win a 12-round unanimous decision over Ray Lampkin for the National American Boxing Federation (NABF) lightweight title. Lampkin demanded a rematch and Esteban beat him again by unanimous decision in July at the Felt Forum in New York. In January of 1974, Esteban knocked out Alfonso (Peppermint) Frazier in 10 rounds and, finally, Roberto Duran agreed to give him a title shot in Panama City in March.

Esteban again started out fast and dropped Duran in the first round of their title fight. Esteban won the early rounds, but Duran came on strong with a vicious body attack in the middle rounds. Duran finally caught up to Esteban and stopped him in the 11th round of their rematch.

After winning several fights in 1974, Esteban decided to move up to the super lightweight division and challenge World Boxing Association champion Antonio Cervantes for the title in May of 1975 in Panama City, Panama. Esteban lost a 15-round unanimous decision to the crafty Cervantes.

Esteban rebounded by knocking out super lightweight contender Rudy Barro in 5 rounds in October and knocked out Valente Ramos in 2 rounds in March of 1976 before dropping down to the lightweight division to challenge World Boxing Council champion Isimatsu (Guts) Suzuki. The title fight with Suzuki was set for May in Bayamon, Puerto Rico.

Esteban finally won a world title in his 3rd attempt as he dominated Suzuki to win a unanimous decision and take his World

Boxing Council lightweight title. Esteban wasted little time in defending his title. He knocked out Hector Medina in 7 rounds in September, and Buzzsaw Yamabe in 6 rounds in February of 1977. In June, Esteban stopped tough Mexican challenger Vicente Mijares in 11 rounds. All of Esteban's title defenses occurred in Bayamon, Puerto Rico. Esteban tuned up for his rubber match with Roberto Duran by winning a unanimous 10-round decision over James Brackett in San Juan.

In January of 1978, Esteban and Duran met in their rubber match in Las Vegas, Nevada to unify the World Boxing Association and World Boxing Council lightweight titles. Esteban again started out fast against the Panamanian legend, but the fight was a carbon copy of their second match as Duran wore Esteban down with a vicious body attack before stopping him in the 12th round.

Esteban fought sporadically after the Duran fight, beating Pablo Baez and Chuchu Hernandez by knockout, and winning a decision over Edwin Viruet to close out 1978. Esteban took a year off from boxing and returned in October of 1979 to win a decision over Jimmy Blevins in New York City. Esteban beat Ruby Ortiz in November and knocked out Jose Vallejo in May of 1980 to set up a title fight with Super Welterweight Champion Saoul Mamby in July.

Esteban started off well but appeared to run out of gas after 10 rounds. Esteban was eventually stopped in the 13th round of the title fight and abruptly retired from the ring. After retirement, it was learned that Esteban had used cocaine with his older brother during the beginning of his professional boxing career.

On Thanksgiving Day in 1980, while under the influence of cocaine, Esteban became involved in a traffic collision with a local 17-year-old Puerto Rican youth, and ended up fatally shooting the youth in the head. Esteban was sentenced to life in prison after the incident. While in prison, Esteban became active in sports and became a born-again Christian in 1984.

In 1985, Esteban had been infected with the HIV virus due to his use of needles when he was doing drugs with his brother. Because of his medical condition the governor of Puerto Rico gave him a pardon to spend his last days with his family. Esteban had become a preacher prior to passing away at the age of 37 in 1989.

It is difficult to say how much the use of drugs effected Esteban's performance in the ring. During the decade of the 1970's he was considered the second best lightweight behind Roberto Duran. His final ring record was 57 or 58 wins (depending on various boxing sources) and 5 losses. He is credited with 32 or 33 knockout victories.

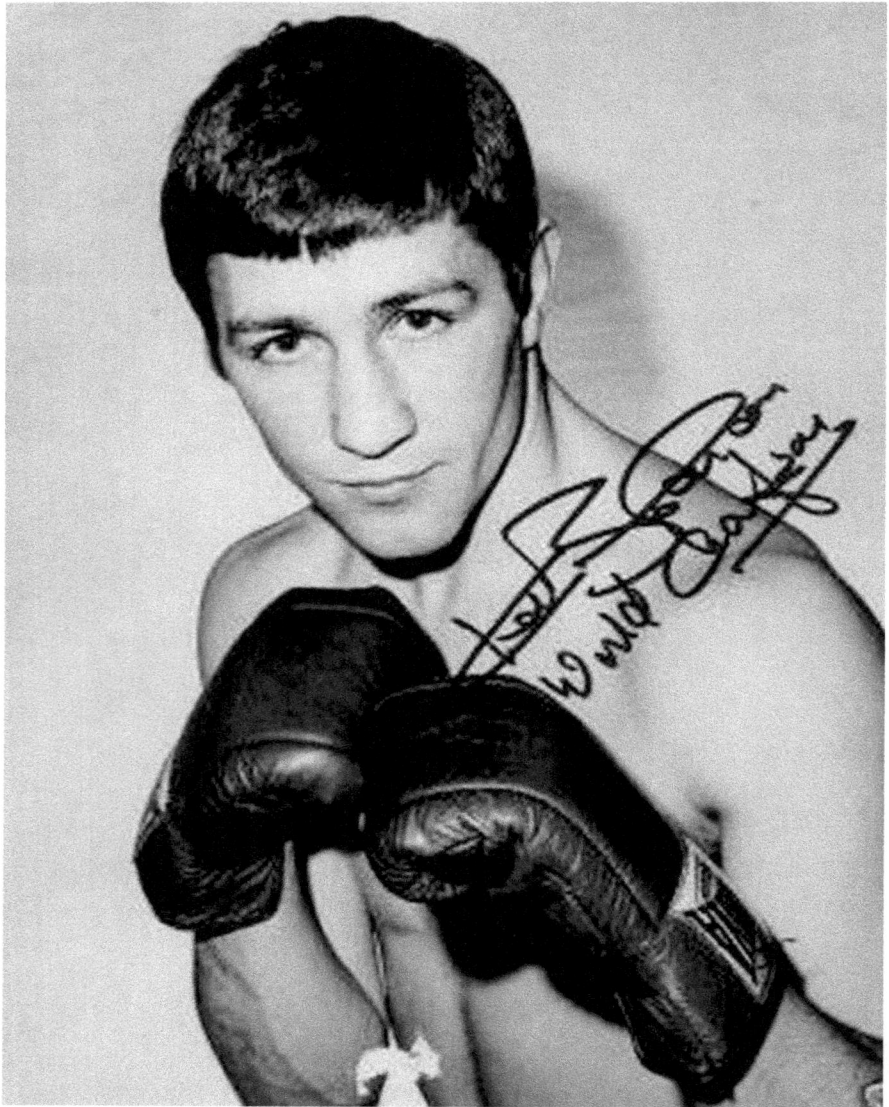

Ken Buchanan

Photograph from BoxRec

Ken Buchanan

Ken Buchanan was born on June 28, 1945, in the historic city of Edinburgh, Scotland. The young Scot was the Amateur Boxing Association featherweight champion before he turned professional in September of 1965 with a 2nd round knockout over Brian Rocky Tonks. Ken was a polished boxer from his amateur days and had one of the best educated left jabs in the business. Ken was a consummate boxer who had an excellent defense, which made it hard for any opponent to beat him.

Ken went undefeated in 1965 with 5 wins, with 4 wins coming by knockout. His opponents were mainly preliminary fighters in his first year of boxing as a professional. Ken plied his trade mostly in London in 1966, and went undefeated in 10 fights before graduating up to 10-round fights at the end of the year.

In January of 1967, Ken returned to Scotland and won the Scottish lightweight title by a 10-round decision over John McMillan in Glasgow. Ken won all 7 of his fights in 1967, closing out the year with a 12-round win over Jim 'Spike' McCormack.

In February of 1968, Ken won the British lightweight title with a 11th round knockout over Maurice Cullen in London. Ken won all 5 of his fights in 1968 and all of his 5 fights in 1969. In January of 1970, Ken suffered his first professional defeat when he lost a 15-round decision to Spaniard, Miguel Velasquez, in a fight held in Madrid, Spain for the European lightweight title.

Ken rebounded from the Velasquez defeat by beating Leonard Tavares and Chris Fernandez by decision, and knocking out Brian Hudson in 5 rounds in defense of his British lightweight title. Ken became the number one ranked contender in the lightweight division and in September he challenged champion Ismael Laguna to a title fight in San Juan, Puerto Rico. The oddsmakers made Laguna the favorite as the fight was to be held in Laguna's home town and it was felt that Ken would not be able to handle the humidity in Puerto Rico.

Ken stunned Laguna and the experts by walking away with the title by using a classic Willie Pep style of boxing to out-speed the champion. Laguna, who was considered a slick boxer, met his match at his own game of boxing. In December, Ken out boxed another slick boxer in Canadian Donato Paduano in a 10-round non-title fight in New York.

In February of 1971, Ken traveled to Los Angeles, California to defend his title against local Mexican fighter Ruben Navarro. Ken put on a masterful boxing exhibition to win a unanimous decision over the local product.

In May, Ken returned to London to knock out Venezuelan knockout artist Carlos Hernandez in 8 rounds at Wembley Stadium. Ismael Laguna asked for a rematch and it was set for Madison Square Garden in New York in September. Ken left no doubt as to who was the better fighter by winning a 15-round unanimous decision over the former champion.

In June of 1972, Ken accepted the challenge of undefeated Panamanian knock out artist Roberto Duran. The fight was held in Madison Square Garden and Ken was the favorite in the fight as Duran was basically unknown outside of his native Panama.

Duran came out aggressively at the start of the fight and had Ken backing up. Ken could not seem to get untracked in the fight against the Panamanian whirlwind. Ken was behind in the scoring in the fight when he was struck by a low blow at the end of the 12th round. Ken was unable to continue and Duran was the new lightweight champion. Ken had a contract for a return match but the irony of it all was that Duran never honored the return bout clause.

Unable to get Duran back into the ring, Ken turned his attention to defending his British lightweight title. In January of 1973, he defended his title by winning a 15-round unanimous decision over future lightweight champion Jim Watt.

In May of 1974, Ken traveled to Italy to knock out Antonio Puddu in 6 rounds to win the European lightweight title. In December, Ken knocked out Leonard Tavarez in 14 rounds in Paris, France, in a European lightweight title defense. In February of 1975, Ken was finally given a shot at the lightweight title against World Boxing Council champion Ishimatsu Suzuki. Ken would have preferred a fight against Duran but he took the fight against Suzuki.

Ken fought an uninspired and listless fight in losing a 15-round decision to the Japanese champion. In July, Ken returned to Italy and knocked out Giancarlo Usai in 12 rounds to defend his European lightweight title. Disgusted at his failed attempts to get Duran back in the ring, he suddenly retired in 1976.

Ken returned to boxing in 1979, and won a couple of comeback fights before he challenged Irishman Charlie Nash for the European lightweight title in December of 1979. Ken had lost a step since his retirement and he lost a 12-round decision to Nash in their championship fight in Copenhagen.

Ken finally retired for good after losing an 8-round decision to club fighter George Feeney in January of 1982.

Since retirement, Ken has battled alcohol problems as well as severe financial issues. It was never quite clear why Roberto Duran never gave Ken a return match. Ken's final ring record was 61 wins and 8 losses. He won 27 fights by knockout. More than half of his losses came after his first retirement. Ken was inducted into the International Boxing Hall of Fame in 2000.

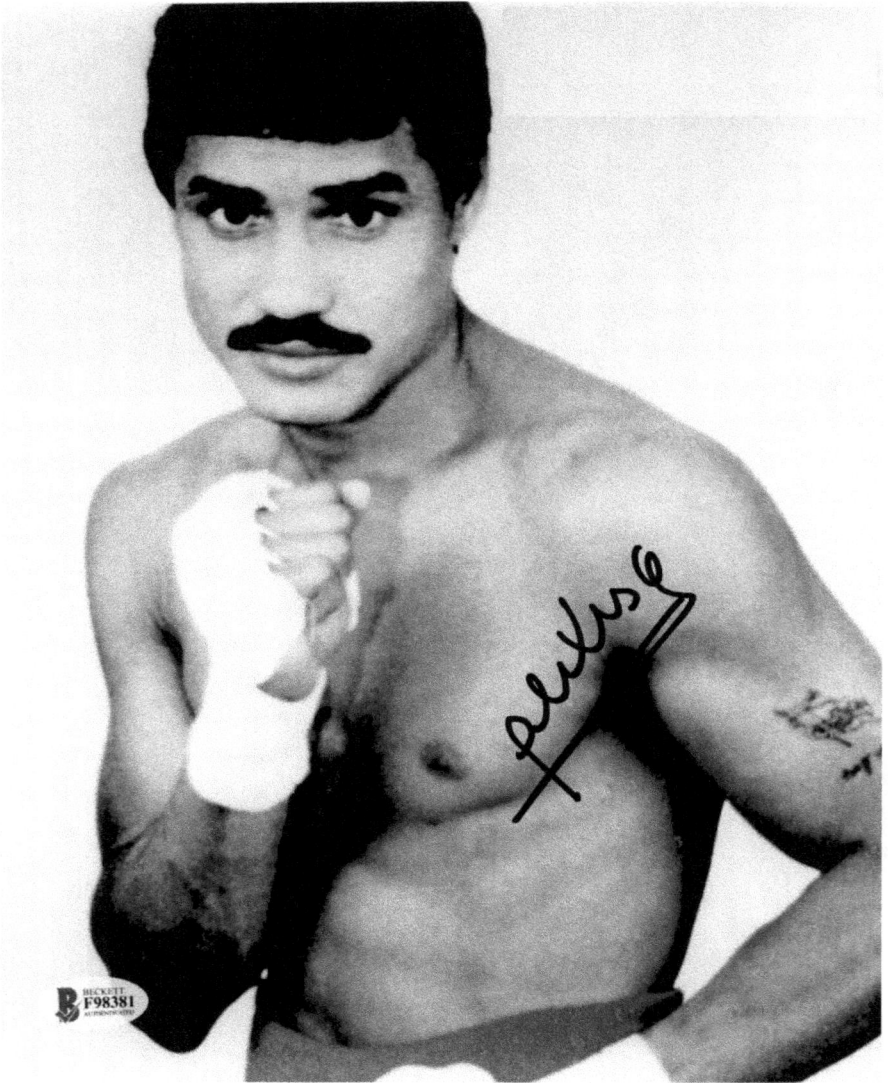

Alexis Arguello

Photograph from Wikipedia

Chapter 6   Top Featherweights of the Decade

Alexis Arguello

Alexis Arguello was born in Managua, Nicaragua on April 19, 1952, into abject poverty. One of his brothers-in-law was a boxer and Alexis took a liking to the sport, building up a reported amateur record of 58 wins with just 2 losses.

He turned professional as a tall (5-10) bantamweight on October 26, 1968, with a knockout over Israel Medina in Nicaragua. Alexis won his first 3 professional fights before he suffered a knockout loss to Omar Amaya in his 4th professional fight. Alexis also lost his 5th professional fight by split decision.

Over the next two years, Alexis would go on a 16-bout win streak which would include him winning the Nicaraguan bantamweight title from Emilio Buitrago in October of 1971.

After suffering a technical knockout loss to Jorge Reyes in January of 1972, Alexis went on a 12-bout winning streak which saw him knock out Octavio (Famoso) Gomez in June and former Featherweight Champion Jose Legra in one round in November.

The victory over Legra earned Alexis a shot at the World Boxing Association featherweight title held by Panamanian Ernesto Marcel. Alexis challenged for the belt in February of 1974, but lost a unanimous 15-round decision to the more experienced and craftier Marcel.

109

Undaunted by his loss to Marcel, Alexis returned to the ring and in May of 1974, he knocked out Canadian Art Hafey in a featherweight title eliminator bout. In August, Alexis won the Central America's featherweight championship when he won a 12-round decision over Oscar Aparicio.

In November of 1974, Alexis again challenged for the World Boxing Association featherweight title when he took on Mexican legend Ruben Olivares. The match was held in the Inglewood Forum in front of Olivares' fanatical supporters.

Olivares started strong and was leading on the scorecards when the two fighters exchanged left hooks in the 13th round. Alexis beat Olivares to the punch with his left hook and, 10 seconds later, Alexis was crowned the new champion of the featherweight division. It was an exciting finish to a fight between two Hall of Fame fighters.

In March of 1975, Alexis traveled to Caracas, Venezuela to stop Leonel Hernandez in 8 rounds in his first successful title defense. In May, Alexis added the vacant Ring magazine and lineal featherweight titles when he stopped Rigoberto Riasco in 2 rounds, in Nicaragua. In October, Alexis traveled to Japan to knock out local favorite Royal Kobayashi in 5 rounds.

Alexis had explosive power in both fists and the press labeled him El flaco Exposivo, which means the explosive thin man in English. In June of 1976, Alexis was back at the Inglewood Forum in California taking on Mexican contender Salvador Torres. Torres was attempting to gain revenge for the Mexican fans for the beating that Alexis had given their hero Ruben Olivares.

Torres had no luck against Alexis as he was stopped in 3 rounds of a one sided fight. Alexis was having a hard time making the 126-pound featherweight limit and, in June of 1977, he vacated his featherweight title. Alexis won all 7 of his fights in 1977, with 6 of his wins coming by knockout. In January of 1978, Alexis attempted to win his second world title when he challenged champion Alfredo Escalera in Bayamon, Puerto Rico.

In a vicious and bloody battle, Alexis stopped Escalera in the 13th round to claim the World Boxing Council super featherweight championship. At the fights end, Escalera's mouth was ripped to shreds and the fight had to be stopped to prevent Escalera from choking on his own blood

In April, Alexis returned to the Inglewood Forum to knock out undefeated challenger Rey Tam in 5 lopsided rounds. In June, Alexis blew out contender Diego Alcala in 1 round in Puerto Rico in an easy title defense before taking on top lightweight contender Vilomar Fernandez in Madison Square Garden in July.

Alexis looked slow afoot and very mechanical as Fernandez pulled out an upset 10-round decision over him. Not to be discouraged Alexis returned to the ring in November and won a unanimous 15-round decision over tough Mexican contender Arturo Leon in Las Vegas

In February of 1979, Alexis gave Alfredo Escalera a rematch for his super featherweight title. Escalera fought a game fight but the outcome was the exact same, as Alexis again stopped him in the 13th round. In July, Alexis returned to New York to take on Rafael (Bazooka) Limon. Alexis chopped up the durable Mexican for a bloody 11th round technical knockout victory.

In November, Alexis returned to one of his favorite venues, the Inglewood Forum, to stop future Hall of Fame fighter Bobby (Schoolboy) Chacon in 7 rounds. In January of 1980, Alexis gave slick boxing Ruben Castillo a shot at his super featherweight title. Castillo started off strong, but Alexis caught up to him in the late rounds to register a 11th round technical knockout victory. In April of 1980, Alexis would defend his title for the last time with a 5th round knockout over hard punching Rolando Navarette in San Juan, Puerto Rico.

Alexis stopped Cornelius Boza-Edwards in August in Atlantic City and then vacated his super featherweight championship to go after the lightweight title. In November, Alexis looked ordinary in winning a split decision over durable Mexican Jose Luis Ramirez. In February of 1981, Alexis returned to top form in blasting out veteran Robert Vasquez in 3 rounds

Alexis challenged World Boxing Council Lightweight Champion Jim Watt for his title in London, England in June of 1981. Watt was a tough fighter from Scotland who had already defeated Olympic gold medalist Howard Davis and Sean O'Grady. Alexis fought a near perfect battle as he won a unanimous decision to gain his third world title. Alexis dropped Watt and totally dominated him from start to finish. Watt's face was badly bruised and he was lucky to last the distance.

In October, Alexis made his first title defense against rugged, undefeated, number one contender Ray (Boom Boom) Mancini. In one of the best fights of the decade, Alexis outlasted Mancini for a 14th round technical knockout victory. Alexis quite correctly predicted after the fight that Mancini would one day become lightweight champion.

Alexis had another tough title defense in May of 1982 when he took on knockout artist Andy Ganigan. Alexis was dropped early in the fight, but he came back to stop Ganigan in the 5th round of a wild brawl. In November of 1982, Alexis attempted to win his 4th world title when he challenged undefeated super lightweight champion Aaron Pryor.

Alexis fought a game battle, and it was a close fight at the end of 13 rounds. Pryor came out for the 14th round energized and stopped Alexis in a classic battle. The fight was controversial as it appeared that Pryor had been given some unknown substance from a bottle that appeared to invigorate him as he came out for the 14th round. A rematch was ordered which would take place the following year.

In February of 1983, Alexis beat Vilomar Fernandez in a rematch and stopped Claude Noel in April. Alexis' rematch with Pryor took place in September of 1983, in Nevada. Pryor again stopped Alexis in the 10th round of a fight lacking controversy. Alexis retired from the ring, but two years later he started a comeback.

In October of 1985, he stopped Pat Jefferson in Anchorage, Alaska, and, in February of 1986, he knocked out Billy Costello in a nationally televised fight. Alexis would again retire and this time his retirement lasted eight years.

Citing financial reasons, Alexis returned to the ring in August of 1994, to win a majority decision over unknown Jorge Palomares. Alexis did not look good in the fight and when he lost to Scott Walker by decision in January of 1995 he retired for good.

Alexis final ring record was 77 wins, and 8 losses. He won 62 fights by knockout. Many boxing experts feel that Alexis may have been the greatest super featherweight champion in boxing history. He never lost any of the 3 world titles that he had won inside of the ring. He had a certain elegance inside and outside of the ring that made him very popular in the boxing community. In 1992, Alex was voted into the International Boxing Hall of Fame.

In the 1980s, Alexis took up arms against the Sandinista Political party. In 2008, he was elected Mayor of Nicaragua as a Sandinista, the same party that he took up arms against in the 1980s. Alexis died on July 1, 2009, of a gunshot wound. It was rumored that he had committed suicide as he had become disenchanted with the Sandinista political party.

Danny (Little Red) Lopez

Photograph from BoxRec

Danny (Little Red) Lopez

Danny (Little Red) Lopez was born on July 6, 1952, in Fort Duchesne, Utah. Danny was a mixture of Indian, Mexican, and Irish descent. He was also the younger brother of former welterweight contender Ernie (Indian Red) Lopez.

Danny lived on a Ute Indian Reservation and in several foster homes before settling in Southern California. Danny looked up to big brother Ernie as he watched him turn professional and challenge twice for the world welterweight title.

Danny turned professional on May 27, 1971, under the guidance of popular Los Angeles trainer Howie Steindler and knocked out Steve Flajole in one round in his pro debut. Danny flashed incredible power in his right hand and knocked out all 8 of his opponents in his first year of professional boxing.

By 1972, Danny was fighting in main events, and he knocked out all 7 of his opponents as his popularity grew in the Los Angeles area with the Latino crowds. Danny continued his knockout spree in 1973 with 6 more knockout victories. Danny continued to fight mainly in Los Angeles, with one knockout victory coming in July in Honolulu, Hawaii.

Danny's 21 bout knockout streak ended in January of 1974, when Genzo Kurosawa extended him the full 10 rounds, before losing a unanimous decision. In February, Danny scored a 10th round come from behind knockout victory over Memo Rodriguez in

115

Mexicali, Mexico to set up a huge cross-town rivalry bout with local unbeaten featherweight, Bobby (School Boy) Chacon.

The fight between the two unbeaten featherweight contenders took place in May in Los Angeles. In a thrilling fight, Chacon turned out to have the better chin as he stopped Danny in the 9th round in a classic ring contest between two future Hall of Fame fighters.

In September, Danny was stopped again in the 9th round as some cut medication used on him between rounds temporarily blinded him and he was unable to continue the fight against Shig Fukuyama. In January of 1975, Danny would lose a 10-round decision to Mexican veteran Octavio (Famoso) Gomez in Anaheim, California.

Danny turned his fortunes around with a 2nd round knockout over veteran Chucho Castillo in April, and a 7th round knockout over Mexican legend Ruben Olivares in December. In February of 1976, Danny stopped unbeaten Sean O'Grady in 4 rounds in Anaheim, California. In April, Danny knocked out Octavio Gomez in a rematch in 3 rounds which set up a featherweight title eliminator match against Canadian Art Hafey. Hafey had been knocking out everyone he had been put up against before the title eliminator fight was set.

In a thrilling contest, Danny outlasted Hafey and eventually stopped him in the 7th round. Danny was now set to challenge World Boxing Council champion David (Poison) Kotey in his native Ghana for the title in December. Unfortunately, his manager Howie Steindler was unable to attend the contest due to failing health.

Danny made the trip to Ghana and beat Kotey so convincingly that he was awarded the unanimous decision and the title in the champion's home country. Kotey received such a beating that he was rushed to the hospital after the contest for medical treatment. It was also reported that many of the rounds only lasted two minutes or whenever Kotey was in danger of being knocked out.

Danny returned to Los Angeles to a hero's welcome but, unfortunately, Howie Steindler would never live to see his fighter defend his title. Steindler was found dead in the backseat of his Cadillac on a Los Angeles freeway in March of 1977. Steindler had been beaten and robbed and to this day it is still an unsolved Los Angeles police homicide case.

Danny won a couple of tune up fights before defending his title against Jose Torres in Los Angeles in September. Local Los Angeles bail bondsman and fight fan, Benny Georgino, took over as the manager of record as Danny stopped Torres in the 7th round of the title fight.

In February of 1978, Danny gave Kotey a rematch for the title in Las Vegas, Nevada. Danny had little problem with Kotey the second time around and stopped him easily in the 6th round of a one-sided fight. Danny's frail looking appearance was deceiving to opponents as he carried unbelievable power in his right hand. Even his jabs were capable of staggering opponents.

Danny defended his title three more times in 1978. He knocked out Brazilian Jose de Paula in 6 rounds in April in Los Angeles, and Argentine Juan Malvarez 2 rounds in September in New Orleans. In October, Danny defeated Fel Clemente by disqualification in a bizarre finish where he sustained major facial cuts due to head butts.

Danny was a huge box office draw due to his incredible punching power and porous defense which made him easy to hit and knock down. Danny had been knocked down on several occasions but he seemed only to get stronger after he had been hurt in a fight. He could be knocked down but keeping him down was much more difficult for his opponents.

In March of 1979, Danny won universal recognition as world featherweight champion when he knocked out Roberto Castanon in 2 rounds in Salt Lake City, Utah. In June, Danny traveled to San Antonio, Texas to take on top challenger Mike Ayala. The fight was a classic with Ayala taking everything that Danny threw at him and then fighting back on even terms. Danny finally caught up to Ayala in the 15th and final round and stopped him for the technical knockout win. Danny's fight with Ayala was one of the top fights of 1979.

In September, Danny had an easy title defense when he stopped Jose Caba in 3 rounds in Los Angeles. In February of 1980, Danny signed to defend his featherweight title against rising Mexican star Salvador Sanchez. The fight was held in Phoenix, Arizona, and it appeared to be another routine title defense for the champion.

Sanchez turned out to be anything but easy as he displayed an iron chin in taking all of Danny's power punches. Sanchez paced himself well in the fight and he came on strong in the second half of the fight to stop Danny in the 13th round. Many boxing observers felt that Danny may have just had an off night and a rematch was scheduled for June in Las Vegas.

Danny put up a brave fight in the rematch, but was again worn down by Sanchez and stopped in the 14th round by the future Hall of Famer. Sanchez's incredible chin and stamina were just too much for Danny to overcome. Danny wisely retired for the first time after this fight.

For some unknown reason Danny returned to the ring in October of 1992 and was knocked out by unknown Jorge Rodriguez in 2 rounds. This turned out to be Danny's last professional fight. Danny's final ring record was 42 wins, 6 losses, with 39 of his wins coming by knockout.

Danny may not have been the very best featherweight champion of the 1970s's but no fighter was more exciting to watch in action. His incredible power and porous defense made for sellout crowds wherever he fought.

In retirement Danny entered into the construction business and lives with his family in Southern California. Danny was inducted into the International Boxing Hall of Fame in 2010.

Eusebio Pedroza

Photograph from BoxRec

Eusebio Pedroza

Eusebio Pedroza was born on March 2, 1956, in Panama City, Panama. He turned professional on December 1, 1973, with a 4th round knockout over Julio Garcia. Fighting exclusively in Panama, Eusebio won his first 9 professional fights before tasting defeat by knockout to Alfonso Perez in January of 1975.

Eusebio went on another winning streak of 5 fights and then challenged World Boxing Association bantamweight champion Alfonso Zamora for the title in April 0f 1976. Zamora was too experienced and powerful and stopped Eusebio in the 2nd round.

Eusebio moved up in weight to the featherweight division and took off on another winning streak of 5 fights before he challenged World Boxing Association champion Cecilio Lastra for the title in April of 1978. In front of his hometown fans in Panama City, Eusebio stopped the game Spaniard in the 13th round to annex the World Boxing Association title.

Eusebio made 2 successful defenses of his title in 1978. In July he stopped Ernesto Herrera in 12 rounds in Panama City and in November he traveled to San Juan, Puerto Rico, to win a unanimous decision over Enrique Solis.

Eusebio was in his prime in 1979 and made he made 4 successful title defenses. In January, he stopped Royal Kobayashi in 13 rounds in Tokyo, and, in April, he knocked out Hector Carrasquilla in 11 rounds in Panama City. Eusebio traveled to

Houston, Texas, in July to knock out Mexican knockout artist Ruben Olivares in 12 rounds. And in November he knocked out undefeated Johnny Aba in 11 rounds in New Guinea.

Eusebio was not a one punch knockout artist like World Boxing Council Featherweight Champion Danny (Little Red) Lopez, but instead he was an accurate combination puncher who wore his opponents down before stopping them in the late rounds.

Eusebio had another banner year in 1980 making 4 more successful title defenses of his featherweight title. In January, he traveled to Tokyo to win a 15-round decision from Spider Nemoto, and in March he stopped perennial Argentine contender Juan Malvarez in 9 rounds in Panama City, Panama. In July, Eusebio traveled to Korea to knock out undefeated Sa-Wang Kim in 8 rounds. In October, Eusebio traveled to McAfee, New Jersey to win a 15-round decision over future super featherweight champion Rocky Lockridge.

No effort was made to match Eusebio with World Boxing Council Featherweight Champion Danny (Little Red) Lopez during his first few years as champion so Eusebio continued on to his record pace of successful World Boxing Association title defenses.

In February of 1981, Eusebio knocked out tough Pat Ford in the 13th round and stopped Venezuelan Carlos Pinango in the 7th round in an August title defense. In December, Eusebio had one of his easier title defenses when he stopped Bashew Sibaca in 5 rounds.

In January of 1982, Eusebio won a tough 15-round decision over future featherweight champion Juan Laporte in a nationally televised fight in New Jersey. Eusebio threw numerous low blows in this fight and, to the national audience, he came across as a dirty fighter. In October, Eusebio defended his title against undefeated Olympian Bernard Taylor in North Carolina. Eusebio did not look good in this fight, and he was lucky to escape with a draw against the awkward Taylor.

In April of 1983, Eusebio gave Rocky Lockridge a rematch in Italy. Eusebio walked away with another unanimous decision over the tough Lockridge. Eusebio won a 15-round decision in April over Jose Caba to close out another year of successful title defenses.

Eusebio slowed down in 1984 and made only one successful defense of his title. He won a 15-round decision over Angel Mayor in Maracaibo, Venezuela, and then prepared to defend against fellow Panamanian Jorge Lujan in February of 1985.

Lujan had been the world bantamweight champion and the fight was a natural for Panama. Eusebio made a record breaking 19 successful defenses of his title when he won a unanimous decision against his fellow Panamanian.

In June, Eusebio accepted a million dollar offer to defend against Irishman Barry McGuigan in London, England. Eusebio looked shop worn in the fight, and McGuigan won a clear cut 15-round unanimous decision to take the featherweight title.

Eusebio fought sporadically after the McGuigan fight, winning 3 fights and losing 2. He finally retired in 1992 with a record of 41 wins, 6 losses, and 1 draw. He won 25 fights by knockout.

Eusebio was a very popular fighter in Latin America but he never quite received the world wide popularity that Alexis Arguello and Danny (Little Red) Lopez enjoyed. A proposed big featherweight unification match with Salvador Sanchez never materialized as Sanchez died in an automobile accident in 1982.

Eusebio was also overshadowed during his career by the legendary fellow Panamanian Roberto Duran. Many American viewers saw him as a dirty fighter because of the nationally televised Juan LaPorte fight.

Popular or not with United States boxing viewers, Eusebio's record speaks for itself as does his 19 successful title defenses. He may have been the best featherweight champion of the 1970's even though he was not the most popular.

Eusebio was inducted into the International Boxing Hall of Fame in 1999. He passed away on March 1, 2019, at the age of 62.

Carlos Zarate

Photograph from BoxRec

Chapter 7   Top Bantamweights of the Decade

Carlos Zarate

Carlos Zarate was born in a suburb of Mexico City, Mexico on May 23, 1951, and was a Mexican Golden Gloves champion, compiling an amateur record of 33 wins, and 3 losses, with 30 wins coming by knockout. At 5-8, Carlos was tall for a bantamweight, and he had tremendous punching power in both fists. He was probably one of the greatest bantamweight body punchers of all time.

Carlos turned professional in 1970, and won his first 23 fights by knockout before Victor Ramirez went the 10-round distance in a January 1974 Mexico City fight. Carlos then went on a 15-bout knockout spree which made him the mandatory challenger for Champion Rodolfo Martinez' World Boxing Council bantamweight title.

Carlos challenged Martinez in May of 1976, at the Inglewood Forum in California. The two Mexican warriors battled it out fiercely but Martinez could not contend with Carlo's fierce body punching and he finally succumbed in the 9th round.

Carlos returned to the Inglewood Forum in August to defend against Australia's top contender, Paul Ferreri. Ferreri put up a courageous battle, but he also wilted under Carlo's vicious body attack in the 12th round of the bantamweight title fight.

In November, Carlos returned to Mexico and stopped Waruinge Nakayama in 4 rounds in Culiacan. In February of 1977, Carlos stopped Fernando Cabanela in 3 rounds in Mexico City. The Mexican boxing fans wanted to see a title unification match between Carlos and World Boxing Association Bantamweight Champion Alfonso Zamora.

The World Boxing Association and the World Boxing Council wanted huge sanctioning fees for the bantamweight showdown, thus the fight was made as a 10-round non-title fight between the two warriors. The fight took place at the Inglewood Forum in May and it was known as the battle between the two Z boys. Both fighters were undefeated knockout artists and the fight was a natural for Southern California.

Carlos had a 6-inch height and reach advantage over Zamora and he put it to good use as he bombed away from long range, rocking the World Boxing Association titleholder in the 2nd and 3rd rounds, before he stopped him in the 4th round. Carlos became the lineal bantamweight champion after this fight.

In October, Carlos returned to Los Angeles to stop Danilo Batista in 6 rounds, and then traveled to Madrid, Spain to knock out Spaniard Juan Francisco Rodriguez in 5 rounds. In February of 1978, Carlos was out boxed by future bantamweight champion Alberto Davila for 5 rounds before he caught up to Davila and slowed him down with body punches for an 8th round knockout. In April, Carlos traveled to San Juan, Puerto Rico and stopped Andres Hernandez in the 13th round of their 15-round title fight. In June, Carlos had an easier time stopping Emilio Hernandez in 4 rounds in Las Vegas, Nevada.

In October, Carlos challenged Puerto Rican Super Bantamweight Champion Wilfredo Gomez in San Juan for his title. Both fighters were big punchers, and it was a cinch that this fight was not going to go the distance. Gomez stunned Carlos first and never let him off the hook. He won by a technical knockout in 5 rounds. Replays of the fight would show that Gomez actually hit Carlos when he was on the floor before his corner threw the towel in. The referee chose to ignore the foul and proclaimed Gomez the winner.

In March of 1979, Carlos would make the last successful defense of his title when he stopped Mensah Kpalongo in 3 rounds in Inglewood, California. Carlos was next challenged for his title by his stablemate, Lupe Pintor.

Carlos defended against Pintor in Las Vegas in June. Even though Carlos was not at his best, most ring analyst felt that he did enough to beat Pintor in the fight. Unfortunately, two of the judges voted for Pintor giving him the title on a split decision. Carlos was incensed by the decision and retired from the ring for close to 7 years.

Carlos returned to the ring in February of 1986 and won a 4-round decision over Adam Garcia. Carlos went on a 12-bout winning streak, which included a 5th round knockout of number one super bantamweight contender Richard Savage.

In October of 1987, Carlos challenged Super Bantamweight Champion Jeff Fenech in Australia for the title. Fenech was given a 4th round technical decision win when it was determined that he was severely cut by a head butt and could not continue the fight. Fenech had been ahead on the scorecards at the time the fight was stopped. Carlos claimed that Fenech was cut by a punch, but the technical decision stood.

In February of 1988, Carlos again challenged for the super bantamweight title when he took on Champion Daniel Zaragoza at the Inglewood Forum in California. Carlos was definitely passed his prime and he was stopped in the 10th round by the younger champion. Carlos retired for good after this bout.

Carlos final ring record was 66 wins, and 4 losses. He won 63 fights by knockout. He had a long and lean body type similar to that of Sandy Saddler and, like Saddler, he had tremendous power in both fists. Carlos was inducted into the International Boxing Hall of Fame in 1994.

Jorge Lujan

Photograph from Sportsandhealth.com.pa

Jorge Lujan

Jorge (Mocho) Lujan was born on March 18, 1965, in Colon, Panama. He signed with manager Aurelio Cortez and started his professional boxing career with a one round knockout of Baby San Blas III in June of 1973, in the Roberto Duran arena.

Cortez honed Jorge's boxing skills and, with a cast iron chin, he went undefeated in his first 15 professional fights against some of the best bantamweights in the division. Jorge's list of victims included Alex Santana, Socrates Batoto, John Cajina, and Reyes Arnal. In May of 1977, Jorge stepped into the ring to face top bantamweight contender Gilberto Illueca. Illueca had just fought Bantamweight Champion Alfonso Zamora for the title.

Illeuca was the favorite in the fight but Jorge showed why he had remained unbeaten in his first 15 fights and lost a controversial 10-round majority decision to the top bantamweight contender. Jorge knocked out Jaime Ricardo in his next fight, and then traveled to Bogota, Colombia to take on Jose Cervantes in September.

Jorge put up a good fight against the top ten bantamweight contender but Cervantes was given the decision after 10 rounds of fighting. World Boxing Association Featherweight Champion Alfonso Zamora had just lost a non-title fight by knockout to Carlos Zarate and he was probably looking for a fairly safe opponent for a title defense. Jorge was available and he got the call to oppose Zamora for the title in November in Los Angeles.

Zamora was trying to regain favor with all of his Mexican fans for his poor performance against Zarate and he was a big favorite in the fight against the unknown Panamanian. Jorge put on a boxing clinic and had Zamora swatting nothing but air before he flashed his power and stopped Zamora in the 10th round to take his World Boxing Association bantamweight title. What punches Zamora did land did not appear to effect Jorge at all.

Mexican boxing fans were shocked at the outcome as Jorge had lost 2 of his previous 3 fights prior to his title bout. The Mexican boxing fans wanted revenge and perennial Mexican contender Roberto Rubaldino was sent to San Antonio, Texas in March of 1978, to try and regain Zamora's old bantamweight title. Jorge entered the ring in front of a hostile Tejano crowd rooting for Rubaldino.

Jorge again put on a masterful boxing exhibition for 10 rounds. Rubaldino was considered a puncher but his blows also seemed to have no effect on Jorge. After Rubaldino had punched himself out, Jorge picked up the pace and stopped his tired Mexican opponent in the 11th round of the title fight.

Jorge stayed on the road to defend his title and his next stop was New Orleans, Louisiana in September as part of the Muhammad Ali versus Leon Spinks boxing card. Jorge's opponent was another slick boxing future bantamweight champion by the name of Alberto (Tweety) Davila. Davila did not have much of a punch but he was considered the slickest boxer in the bantamweight division.

In a classic match between two masterful boxers, Jorge proved that not only was he the best boxer in the division, but that he could also punch as he took a unanimous decision from Davila. Jorge picked up the lineal championship also after his mastery over Davila.

Jorge took 7 months off from boxing and did not defend his title again until April of 1979. Jorge's title challenger was tough

Nicaraguan, Cleo Garcia. Garcia did not have a good record but he could punch, and he had just knocked out his last 4 opponents.

Jorge showed no effects from the 7-month layoff as he boxed superbly and went all out in the 15th and final round to stop the tired challenger for the knockout. Jorge was not a flashy fighter but he combined excellent boxing skills with incredible stamina and a rock-solid chin.

Roberto Rubaldino asked for a rematch in Texas and Jorge granted his wish. The rematch took place in McAllen, Texas in October. Rubaldino vowed that the rematch would be different and that he would be the new champion. Rubaldino put up a better fight in the rematch but he was also stopped by Jorge in the 15th and final round of their title fight.

Jorge took another layoff from boxing and did not defend his title again until April of 1980. Jorge traveled to Tokyo, Japan to defend against popular local fighter Shuichi Isogami. Jorge started off faster in this title defense as he did not wish to wait until the last round to stop his opponent. Jorge finished off his Japanese opponent in the 9th round of the Tokyo title fight.

In August, Jorge defended against unbeaten top ranked Puerto Rican contender Julian Solis in Miami Beach. The 15-round fight was very close and most ringside observers felt that Jorge had retained his title. The Panamanian judge gave the fight to Jorge and the Puerto Rican judge gave the nod to Solis. The American referee Jimmy Rondeau gave the fight to Solis by one point. Solis was the new champion in a fight that many boxing fans felt was too close to take away a fighter's championship.

Jorge sought another chance at the World Boxing Association title and challenged new champion Jeff Chandler in January of 1981. Jorge fought a game fight to last the distance in losing a 15-round unanimous decision.

In 1982, Jorge moved up to the super featherweight division, and challenged the champion Sergio Palma. Jorge lost another 15-round decision and appeared to be ready to retire from the ring. Jorge won a couple of fights in 1983 and then upset top ranked Ricardo Cardona in June of 1984 to earn a shot at the featherweight title held by Eusebio Pedroza.

In February of 1985, Jorge lost a decision to Pedroza in Panama in his last title fight. In December, Jorge lost a split decision to top ranked Jose Marmolejo and retired from the ring. Jorge never returned to the ring and his final record was 27 wins, and 9 losses. He won 16 fights by knockout and he was never knocked out in his ring career.

Jorge was a skilled ring technician who fought all the great fighters of the day. Many of his losses were close, or disputed. He defended his bantamweight title all over the world, and, for the most part, he was overshadowed in his career by Roberto Duran and Eusebio Pedroza. He was most definitely one of the best bantamweights of the 1970s.

Ruben Olivares

Photograph from utube.com

Ruben Olivares

Ruben Olivares was born on January 14, 1947, in Mexico City, Mexico. Ruben turned professional at the age of 17 by knocking out Freddy Garcia in February of 1964. Ruben proceeded to knock out his first 22 opponents until he was taken the 10-round distance by Felipe Gonzalez in March of 1967. Two fights later, German Bastidas held Ruben to a majority draw.

In November of 1967, Ruben knocked out Felipe Gonzalez and in January of 1968, he knocked out German Bastidas in return matches. In March of 1968, Ruben received a world ranking in the bantamweight division when he stopped former world flyweight champion Salvatore Burruni in 3 rounds.

Ruben continued his climb up the bantamweight rankings by stopping contenders Octavio (Famoso) Gomez in June of 1968, and Jose Medel in November. In May of 1969, Ruben knocked out Takao Sakurai in a bantamweight elimination match.

Ruben received his first shot at the bantamweight title when he faced world champion Lionel Rose from Australia in August of 1969. The match was held at the Inglewood Forum in California, in front of a packed house of his Mexican fans. Ruben entered the ring unbeaten in 52 professional fights. Rose was an aborigine boxer from down under who had recently successfully defended his title against fan favorite, Chucho Castillo. The decision Rose received over

139

Castillo was unpopular with Mexican fight fans and they were screaming for Ruben to avenge Castillo's defeat.

Ruben did not leave the outcome of the fight in the judges' hands as he stopped Rose in the 5th round with his withering body attack. Ruben became a national hero in Mexico and his aggressive style of fighting and his vicious body punching is what his fans loved about him.

A knockout and a sold-out crowd was expected at every Olivares fight and Ruben did not disappoint his fans when he defended his title by knocking out England's Alan Rudkin in 2 rounds in December of 1969.

In April of 1970, Ruben defended against arch rival Chucho Castillo. Castillo was a rugged competitor who also had a knockout punch. Ruben had to get off of the floor to fight hard to win a close decision against Castillo. The fight was competitive and Castillo and the fans wanted to see a rematch.

Ruben tuned up for the rematch by winning 3 non-title fights. The rematch was set for October of 1970 at the Inglewood Forum again. Ruben had the misfortune of suffering a cut in the very first round. Ruben had to fight an uphill battle and the fight was finally stopped in the 14th round because of his cut. The closeness of the first two fights automatically called for a rubber match between these two Mexican warriors.

The rubber match took place in April of 1971 at the Inglewood Forum. As in the first match, Ruben had to get off of the floor to come back and take a unanimous decision over Castillo in another slugfest. At this point in his career, Ruben was probably more popular than the President of Mexico and he began an acting career in his home country. When not making movies, Ruben still found time to score non-title knockout victories in fights from May to August of 1971.

In October, Ruben found time to defend his title and traveled to Japan to meet Kazuyoshi Kanazawa. Ruben administered a severe body beating to the Japanese challenger before knocking him out in the 14th round. In December, Ruben returned to the Inglewood Forum to take on perennial top ten contender Jesus Pimentel. Pimentel's manager, Harry Kabakoff, had maintained that Ruben was "ducking" his fighter. Ruben gave Pimentel a systematic beating before stopping him in the 11th round to silence Kabakoff and his critics.

In March of 1972, Ruben returned to Mexico and lost his title to countryman Rafael Herrera on an 8th round technical knockout. After the Herrera fight, reports began coming out of Mexico that Ruben had been living "the high life" and not training properly for his fights. He was also finding it difficult to make the bantamweight limit of 118 pounds. After losing a 10-round non-title fight rematch with Herrera in November, Ruben decided to move up to the featherweight division

In June of 1973, Ruben stopped future Hall of Famer Bobby Chacon in 9 rounds and proved that he could also be a force in the featherweight division. He was surprisingly stopped by Canadian Art Hafey in 5 rounds in September but won their rematch by 12-round decision in March of 1974.

In July, Ruben knocked out Zensuke Utagawa in 7 rounds to win the vacant World Boxing Association featherweight title. In a battle of Hall of Fame fighters, Ruben was stopped by Alexis Arguello in the 13th round of their title fight in November. Ruben was ahead in the fight until he ran out of gas and was knocked out.

Ruben received another chance at the featherweight title when he took on World Boxing Council champion Bobby Chacon in a rematch in June of 1975. Chacon really lost his title on the scales when he had to lose over 20 pounds in the last few days before the fight to make the 126-pound featherweight limit. Ruben easily knocked out the physically weakened Chacon in the 2nd round of the fight.

Ruben lost his featherweight title in his first defense against African David (Poison) Kotey by split decision in September. Ruben was also stopped by future featherweight champion Danny (Little Red) Lopez in December.

Ruben lost a decision to old foe Bobby Chacon in August of 1977. After the Chacon fight Ruben went on a 6-fight winning streak which led him to challenge Eusebio Pedroza for the World Boxing Association featherweight title in July of 1979. Ruben was stopped by Pedroza in the 12th round in, what would be, his last world title fight.

Ruben would fight infrequently until 1988 when he was stopped by Ignacio Madrid and retired for good from the ring with a record of 89 wins, 13 losses, and 3 draws. He won 79 fights by knockout. He was a tremendous puncher who went on two knockout sprees of over 20 fights in a row during his career. Ruben was generally recognized as Mexico's greatest fighter, until Julio Cesar Chavez came along in the 1980's. He became famous in Mexico not only for his boxing skills but also as an actor in the Mexican film industry. He was inducted into the International Boxing Hall of Fame in 1991.

Miguel Canto

Photograph from BoxRec

Chapter 8   Top Flyweights of the Decade

Miguel Canto

Miguel Canto, the man known as "the little maestro", was born in Merida in the Yucatan province of Mexico on January 30, 1948. Miguel turned to boxing because his family was desperately poor, and he was one of the few legendary fighters to lose his professional debut. Not only did he lose his professional debut by knockout in February of 1969, he was unceremoniously knocked out by Raul Hernandez in the 3rd round in front of his hometown fans in Merida.

Miguel was knocked out in his 3rd professional fight, and by the end of 1969 his professional boxing record was a mediocre 2 wins, and 2 losses. Miguel then went on a 7-fight winning streak which included 2 wins over fellow local flyweight Vicente Pool. Miguel was matched with Pool for the 3rd time for the Yucatan flyweight title in May of 1970.

Miguel continued his mastery over Pool by winning the Yucatan title with a 12-round unanimous decision. Miguel won all 12 of his bouts in 1971 before he challenged Rocky Garcia in January of 1972 for the Mexican flyweight title. Miguel won a unanimous decision to take the Mexican title and crack the top ten in world flyweight rankings.

In May, Miguel defended his title against Ricardo Delgado in Merida. Miguel won a unanimous decision and was victorious in all

7 seven of his fights for the year. Miguel climbed to the top of the flyweight ratings in 1973 with wins over Tarcisio Gomez and Chamaco Rodriguez before challenging Venezuelan World Champion Betulio Gonzalez.

Miguel fought Gonzalez for the title in August in Caracas, Venezuela. In a close fight, Miguel lost a 15-round majority decision to the Venezuelan champion. Miguel regrouped and won all 5 of his fights in Mexico in 1974 before challenging World Boxing Council Flyweight Champion Shoji Oguma for the title in January of 1975.

Miguel took the title from Oguma by a majority 15-round decision in Japan. In May, Miguel defended his title against Betulio Gonzalez in a rematch. Miguel took a 15-round split decision from the Venezuelan in Nuevo Leon, Mexico. In August, Miguel stopped Jiro Takeda in the 11th round of their title fight in Merida. This would be the only title defense that Miguel would win by knockout.

In a December title defense, Miguel defeated Ignacio Espinal by unanimous decision in Merida. In May of 1976, Miguel won another unanimous decision over Japanese challenger Susumu Hanagata in his hometown. In October, Miguel traveled to Caracas for his rubber match with former champion Betulio Gonzalez. Miguel and Gonzalez were probably the two best flyweights of the decade. Miguel won the first 3 rounds with his left jab and countering right crosses. Gonzalez came back to win the 4th through 7th rounds using his height and reach advantage with his aggressive style. From the 8th through the 12th rounds the fight was fought on even terms. Miguel consistently beat Gonzalez to the punch in the last 3 rounds to win decisively to take a split decision in the challenger's hometown.

In November, Miguel fought in the United States for the first time when he defended his title and beat Orlando Javierto by decision in Los Angeles, California. In April of 1977, Miguel was back in Caracas to successfully defend his title against local challenger Reyes Arnal by decision.

In June, Miguel returned to Tokyo to win a unanimous decision from Kimio Furesawa. In September, Miguel defended his title against Chile's Martin Vargas in Merida. Miguel won a close decision over Vargas and gave him a return match in November in Santiago, Chile. The result was the same, with Miguel taking another 15-round decision over the Chilean challenger.

Miguel defended his title 3 times in 1978. In January, he won a close split decision over Shoji Oguma in Japan. Miguel traveled back to Japan in April to give Oguma a rematch. Miguel won a decisive unanimous decision to prove his superiority over his game Japanese challenger. In November, Miguel took a split 15-round decision over challenger Facomron Vibonchai in Houston, Texas.

In February of 1979, Miguel successfully defended his title for the 14th time when he took a unanimous decision over Antonio Avelar in Merida. Miguel's luck ran out when he lost his title to Chan Hee Park by unanimous decision in Pusan, South Korea in March. In September, Miguel returned to South Korea in an attempt to regain his title. His rematch with Park was ruled a majority draw. The rematch with Park would be Miguel's last world title fight.

Miguel would win both of his fights in 1980, and he would split a couple of decisions with Gabriel Bernal in 1981. After 3 consecutive knockout losses, Miguel retired from the ring in July of 1982 with a final ring record of 61 wins, 9 losses, and 4 draws. He won 15 fights by knockout.

Miguel was the best flyweight of the 1970s and probably within the top 3 of all time. At barely 5 feet tall, and around 110 pounds in the ring, he was a defensive master and great counterpuncher. He had incredible stamina, and he defended his title numerous times and was famous all over the world. He was a legend in a country which was enamored with power and body punching in the ring. He was often compared in skill to the old-time ring master, Willie Pep. Miguel was inducted into the International Boxing Hall of Fame in 1998.

Masao Ohba

Photograph from BoxRec

Masao Ohba

Masao Ohba was known as the "eternal champion" due to his untimely death at the age of 23 while still the reigning flyweight champion in 1973. Masao was born into poverty on October 21, 1949, in Tokyo, Japan. He was born into poverty partly because of a compulsive gambling father. By the time Masao turned to professional boxing to escape poverty in 1966, he had grown to 5 feet 6 inches tall and usually had a height and reach advantage over most of his flyweight opponents.

Masao fought almost exclusively in Tokyo for the first 2 years of his career and was trained by Isamu Kuwata. Masao had a record of 16 wins, 1 loss, and 1 draw when he lost his first 10-round fight to world ranked Susumu Hanagata in September of 1968.

Masao became a top contender for the flyweight title when he defeated World Boxing Association Flyweight Champion Bernabe Villacampo in a 10-round non-title fight in Tokyo in December of 1969. Thailand's Berkrerk Chartvanchai defeated Villacampo for the title in April of 1970 in Bangkok, and he agreed to make his first title defense against Masao in Tokyo in October of 1970. It would be one of the few times in his career Masao did not have a height or reach advantage over his opponent.

Masao boxed well and then overpowered the weakened champion in the 13th round with a volley of head punches to win the title. Chartvanchai stated after the fight that he had been weakened by a cut he received in the fight and by trying to make the flyweight limit of 112 pounds. The ex-champion would never fight in another world title fight.

Masao tuned up for his first title defense by stopping Switzerland's Fritz Chervet in 8 rounds in January of 1971. He made his first title defense against future 3-time world flyweight champion Betulio Gonzalez from Venezuela in April in Tokyo. Masao boxed beautifully to take a convincing 15-round unanimous decision over the tough Venezuelan.

In June, Masao traveled to San Antonio, Texas to knockout Rocky Garcia in 9 rounds of a non-title fight. This would be Masao's only appearance in the United States. Masao made the 2nd defense of his title against the Philippine's Fernando Cabanella in October of 1971. Masao thrashed Cabanella to win a 15-round unanimous decision in front of his hometown Tokyo fight fans.

In March of 1972, Masao defended against Japanese challenger Susumu Hanagata. Hanagata had previously defeated Masao by decision in 1968. The fight was held in Tokyo in front of a packed house. It was a close and difficult fight for Masao and he was lucky to escape with a 15-round majority decision win. Hanagata would continue on to become flyweight champion for a brief time in 1974.

In June, Masao defended against tough Cuban Orlando Amores in Tokyo. Masao flashed his power and stopped the overmatch Cuban in the 5th round for his 4th successful title defense. As was his custom, Masao took a tune up fight before his 5th and final title defense. Masao stopped Natalio Jimenez in 5 rounds before deciding to defend against former world flyweight champion Chartchai Chionoi in January of 1973. Chionoi had been flyweight champion from 1966 to 1969, and he would not be an easy opponent for Masao. The fight was to be held in Tokyo, like all of the champion's title defenses

Chionoi dropped Masao with a hook in the opening round, and the champion injured his ankle falling to the floor. Masao barely survived the opening round and limped through the next few rounds. By the 8th round, Masao was battling Chionoi on even terms as the challenger began to tire from Masao's steady attack of body and head blows. Masao dropped Chionoi to the canvas 3 times in the 12th round with right hands before the referee stopped the fight. The win over Chionoi made Masao a perfect 6 wins and 0 losses in world title fights.

Masao was finding it difficult to make the 112-pound flyweight limit, and he was considering a move up to the 118-pound bantamweight limit. Taking a break from training after the Chionoi fight, Masao bought a brand new 1973 Corvette sports car and a new home for his parents.

Masao just had his driver's license for several months before he bought his Corvette sports car. On January 24, 1973, he was driving his Corvette when it jumped a dividing lane outside of Tokyo and hit a parked truck on the opposite side of the road. Masao died in the one car accident at the age of 23 as the reigning world flyweight champion.

Masao's final ring record was 35 wins, 2 losses, and 1 draw. He won 16 fights by knockout. He was already a great champion at the time of his death, and it is conceivable that he would probably had gone on to become a champion in the bantamweight division. Masao was inducted into the International Boxing Hall of Fame in 2015.

Erbito Salavarria

Photograph from Pinterest.com

Erbito Salavarria

Erbito Salavarria was born on January 20th, 1946, in Manilla, Philippines. He turned professional in June of 1963 with a 4-round decision win over Johnny Bulawan. Erbito went undefeated until his 10th professional fight when Johnny Bulawan won a 10-round decision over him in a rematch in October of 1964.

Erbito went on another winning streak of 7 fights until he was stopped by Al Diaz in the 9th round in April of 1966 in Manila. Erbito won his next 2 fights and then challenged veteran Ric Magramo for the Philippines flyweight title. The more experienced Magramo won a 12-round decision over Erbito in November.

In May of 1967, Erbito took on Magramo in a rematch in Manila. Erbito took the title from Magramo with a 12-round split decision win. Eribito fought a rubber match with Magramo in October and lost his title on a 12-round decision.

In August of 1968, Erbito and Magramo fought for the 4th and final time. Erbito evened the series at 2 wins and 2 losses when he won a 12-round majority decision to take back his Filipino title. In May of 1969, Erbito defended his title in a rematch with Al Diaz. Erbito won a 12-round decision over Diaz in Quezon City, Philippines.

In October of 1969, Erbito won the Oriental flyweight title with a 12th round knockout over Tsuyoshi Nakamura in Manila. Erbito had a break out year in 1970 as he gained the world championship by the end of the year. In March, he defended his Oriental title by knocking out Shigeru Taremizu in Tokyo in 2 rounds, and in June he won a 12-round decision over Wittaya Pleonjit in another Oriental flyweight title defense. In July, Eribito won a 10-round non-title decision over World Boxing Association Flyweight Champion Berkerk Chartvanchai

In December, Erbito flew to Bangkok, Thailand to challenge World Boxing Council Flyweight Champion Chartchai Chionoi. Erbito shocked Chionoi and thousands of his Thailand fans when he knocked the champion out in the 2nd round to annex his world flyweight title.

In April of 1971, Erbito made his first title defense against top ranked Japanese challenger Susumu Hanagata. Eribito out boxed Hanagata to take the 15-round unanimous decision. In November, Erbito flew to Venezuela to take on local Betulio Gonzalez.

Erbito's fight with Gonzalez was close and controversial. The fight was proclaimed a draw after 15 rounds, but the Gonzalez camp claimed that Erbito drank some illegal substance during the fight, and that he should be disqualified. Eribito claimed that he just drank a mixture of water and honey in between rounds given to him by a corner man.

In strictly a political move, the World Boxing Council chose to strip Eribito of his title due to the complaint lodged by the Gonzalez camp. In today's world, the fight would have probably been called a no contest and Erbito would have kept his title.

Eribito returned to the Philippines in August of 1972 and successfully defended his Oriental title with a 12-round decision win over Dong Ki Cho. In February of 1973, Erbito traveled to Bangkok and lost a 15-round world title fight decision against Venice Borkhorsor.

In 1974, Erbito won 2 of his 3 fights before traveling to Japan to challenge World Boxing Association Flyweight Champion Susumu Hanagata in April of 1975. Erbito had defeated Hanagata in a successful title defense in 1971 in Manila. Erbito gave Hanagata a boxing lesson in front of his fans to become world champion for the second time with a 15-round decision win. Hanagata asked for a rematch and Erbito gave him one in Japan again in October. The result was the same with Erbito winning another 15-round decision over his Japanese challenger.

In February of 1976, Erbito lost his title when he was stopped in the 15th and final round by undefeated challenger Alfonso Lopez in Manila. Erbito did not fight again until December of 1978 when he was stopped by Netrnoi Sor Vorasingh in Bangkok. Erbito retired after this fight and his final ring record was 40 wins, 11 losses, and 3 draws. He won 11 fights by knockout.

Erbito was a classy boxer who exhibited good stamina in the ring. He was not a knockout puncher, but he did not need to be to defeat the top-rated flyweights of his day. During his career he fought in Venezuela, the Philippines, United States, Japan, Mexico, Thailand, and Panama.

Eribito became a successful business man in the Philippines, and trained fighters and owned a gym. In 2018, Erbito was inducted into the Philippines Sports Hall of Fame.

Chapter 9   *Boxing's Hall of Fame*

Boxing has never had a Hall of Fame as established as the Baseball Hall of Fame, in Cooperstown New York, or the Professional Football Hall of Fame, in Canton, Ohio. The Naismith Professional Basketball Hall of Fame in Springfield, Massachusetts is also probably more established then boxing's halls of fame.

Nat Fleischer introduced his list of Hall of Fame fighters in his Ring Magazine in 1954. Since the Ring's hall of fame listings, a World Boxing Hall of Fame was started in the Los Angeles, California area by Everett Sanders in 1980. Professional boxers were inducted every year and it became a gala event of sorts in Southern California. The World Boxing Hall of Fame never really had a permanent home and it basically died out around 2010. The World Boxing Hall of Fame was riddled by mismanagement and was shut down by threats of a law suit. Some of the members on the board were inducting themselves into their own Hall and the organization began to lose credibility.

Former welterweight contender Armando Muniz was presiding over the World Boxing Hall of Fame board when it was shut down. Muniz was conveniently inducted into his group's Hall of Fame and a fighter who had won three world championships, like Sacramento, California's Tony (The Tiger) Lopez was never considered for induction. Such inconsistencies help cast a shadow over the integrity over the organization. As of this date, they have not had an induction ceremony since 2010 and their trophies are stored somewhere in a storage area in Riverside, California

The most recent Hall of Fame was started in 1990 and is called the International Boxing Hall of Fame. It was started by a local named Ed Brophy with land donated by former welterweight and middleweight boxing champion Carmen Basilio in Canastota, New York.

Though it is currently the most successful Boxing Hall of Fame, it is still a far cry from the Halls of Fame in the other major sports, such as baseball, football, and basketball. A few short years ago the International Boxing Hall of Fame suffered a burglary where ex-middleweight champion Tony Zale's and Carmen Basilio's donated championship belts were stolen. To my knowledge I do not know if the prestigious and priceless championship belts have ever been recovered. I have never heard of such an occurrence happening at the other major sports Halls of Fame. Reportedly, no security cameras were installed at the time of the thefts in 2015.

The selection of boxers in the modern categories for induction into the International Boxing Hall of Fame have been decent. So far, the executives and board members have not inducted themselves into their Hall of Fame to my knowledge. The biggest problem with the International Boxing Hall of Fame is that their selection process lacks transparency. According to ESPN writer Dan Rafael, the International Boxing Hall of Fame never publishes vote totals for the nominated fighters, and it is not necessary for a boxer to get 75 per cent of the vote total to get inducted into their Hall of Fame, such as baseball requires. The top three boxers nominated who get the most votes get inducted regardless of their vote total, thus ensuring an induction ceremony every year, no matter how bad the induction pool is. Theoretically, a boxer could get as little as 10 to 20 per cent of the writers votes and still get inducted into the Hall of Fame. As you can see Major League Baseball has much higher standards for entry into their Hall of Fame.

The International Boxing Hall of Fame has inducted actor Sylvester Stallone into their Hall of Fame, which I could understand due to his popularizing boxing with his Rocky movies. Carmen Basilio who donated the land for the Hall of Fame is also a most deserving inductee. In fact, in my opinion, I believe Basilio to be the best professional welterweight fighter of the 1950's decade.

What would be examples of signs that the International Boxing Hall of Fame has lost credibility? Ed Brophy inducting himself in the Hall of Fame would be an example. The induction of Sylvester Stallone's lesser known brother Frank Stallone, solely because of family connections, and his special interests in boxing and collector status would be another. Another poor choice would be Basilio's nephew Billy Backus who lives in the Canastota area and won the welterweight championship from Jose Napoles on a fluke, and incurred 20 losses in his ring career.

The weakest part of the selection process for induction into the International Boxing Hall of Fame is in the old timers' categories, specifically in the late era section of boxers whose last bout was no earlier than 1943 or later than 1988.

The selection weakness in this area is largely due to the voting of the Boxing Writers Association of America (BWAA) or who should be more aptly named the Blogging Writers Association of America. The on-line bloggers of America are frequently unaware of who these old-time boxers are and it shows in their balloting. Trust me you will not find a writer such as the legendary New York writer Jimmy Cannon in this organization.

Actually, the International Boxing Hall of Fame is more of a National Boxing Hall of Fame. Many great South American fighters are excluded from entry. The group known as the Black Murderer's Row is well known as they fought in the United States and their exploits are recognized and they have deservedly been inducted into the Boxing Hall of Fame. However, legends in South America like

Mauro Mina in Peru, Eduardo Lausse in Argentina, and Betulio Gonzalez in Venezuela are seldom considered for membership into the Hall of Fame. Until these South American legends are inducted into the Hall of Fame, it will never be considered a true International Boxing Hall of Fame.

The most qualified and knowledgeable boxing group to vote on the old timers' sections should be the Members of the International Boxing Research Organization (IBRO). This group has worldwide members that research and try to verify and update fighters' records. If this group cannot verify that a fight has taken place, they adjust the boxer's record.

Once upon a time ex middleweight champion Joey Giardello was credited with 100 victories. Now, I believe, he is listed as having 98 victories on his record. At this point Rocky Marciano is undefeated with 49 wins to his credit. I only hope that his record is not somehow reduced to show only 46 wins on his record in the near future. Hopefully this group will not research the Bible or it may end up being the shortest book ever written if any verifications cannot be made. I have now included a list of a fighter in each major weight division that I feel should immediately be inducted into the International Boxing Hall of Fame.

Primo Carnera

Photograph from BoxRec

Fighters Who Should Be in the International Boxing Hall of Fame

Chapter 10   Heavyweight

Primo Carnera

Primo Carnera should be in the Hall of Fame. Probably a lot of you readers are laughing now, but I am serious. What you should probably be laughing about is that former heavyweight champion Ingemar Johannson is in the International Boxing Hall of Fame. I am sure you remember the big Swede. He is a guy that caught glass chinned Floyd Patterson one summer night in 1959 with a right hand and won the title.

After old Ingemar won the title, he proceeded to get knocked out in a rematch with Patterson and lose the title the following year. Ingemar also managed to get himself knocked out by Patterson in the rubber match and by 1961, he was gone from the United States boxing scene. After a few meaningless victories in Europe, he quietly retired from boxing for good. Now, how is that for International Boxing Hall of Fame credentials? So, let's set the bar at Johannsen's credentials for getting into the International Boxing Hall of Fame.

Let's talk now about old Primo Carnera, who, in my opinion, has much better credentials then Ingemar to get into the Hall of Fame. Primo was born on October 25, 1906, in Sequals, Italy. By age

14, he had moved to France and, due to his large size, he appeared as a circus strongman in a traveling circus.

Primo was eventually introduced to French promoter Leon See who saw a great potential in exploiting his size to draw large crowds to boxing matches. Primo had grown close to 6 feet 6 inches in height by the time he made his professional debut September 12, 1928, in Paris, France. Primo was basically a cumbersome novice who had virtually no training at all in boxing when he entered the ring. By sheer strength Primo knocked out the more experienced Leon Sebilo in 2 rounds

Primo went undefeated in his first 6 fights, and by his 4th fight he was fighting in 10-round fights. In his 7th professional fight, he managed to get himself disqualified in Germany. Despite being ill trained, Primo still managed to defeat 14 of his first 15 hand-picked opponents by his sheer strength, size, and fear.

In November of 1929, Primo was matched with future Hall of Fame light heavyweight Young Stribling in London, England. Primo managed a flash knockdown in the 3rd round, but by the 4th round he was being badly out boxed by Stribling. Primo went down in the 5th round claiming a foul and he was awarded a disqualification win in a fight he was about to lose.

Primo and Stribling had a rematch a month later in Paris. This time it was Primo's turn to get disqualified as he struck Stribling in the back of the head after the bell ending the 7th round. Primo's fights with Stribling drew interest from American boxing promoters who saw Primo as a huge gate attraction even though he was not a legitimate heavyweight contender yet.

Primo's managers of record in the United States were Louis Soreci and Bill Duffy, but, unfortunately, some New York underworld figures entered into the promotional team, and it was felt that some of his early fights in the United States were fixed, or I guess you could call it pre-arranged endings

An obvious example of one of the pre-arranged fights occurred when legitimate heavyweight contender George Godfrey was mysteriously disqualified in a June of 1930 match in Philadelphia. Godfrey won the first 4 rounds handily, and then was disqualified in the 5th when he had Primo in serious trouble

In October, Primo lost a 10-round decision to heavyweight contender Jim Maloney in Boston. In losing to Maloney, Primo showed some legitimate boxing skills as he was gaining in experience. In November, Primo went to Barcelona, Spain and was given a 10-round decision over local heavyweight contender Paulino Uzcuden. The fight attracted 75,000 fans, and the fight was close even though many thought Uzcuden should have received the decision.

In March of 1931, Primo fought a rematch with Jim Maloney in Miami, Florida. For the first time, Primo fought an excellent fight against a top contender and won a convincing 10-round decision. Primo continued to beat non-contenders until he was matched with future heavyweight champion Jack Sharkey in October of 1931. Sharkey won the 15-round decision but Primo showed heart and some skill in lasting the 15-round distance.

In November, Primo upset King Levinsky with a 10-round decision, and became a top contender for the heavyweight title in 1932 when he scored victories over Levinsky in a rematch and a 10-round newspaper decision win over Californian Art Lasky.

In February of 1933, Primo fought top contender Ernie Schaaf in an elimination match to determine a challenger for heavyweight champion Jack Sharkey. Schaaf entered the ring in a somewhat weakened condition by the flu before the fight and he looked listless. Primo battered Schaaf during the fight and in the 13th round knocked him down with what looked like a long, left jab. Schaaf fell to the canvas along the ropes and could not get up. Primo was awarded a 13th round knockout victory, and Schaaf died several days later at a New York hospital. Some boxing critics called for a super heavyweight division to accommodate Primo's large size. Other critics claimed that Schaaf had already sustained a brain injury from previous fights.

In June of 1933, Primo challenged champion Jack Sharkey in Long Island, New York for the title. Sharkey had won a convincing 15-round decision over Primo in their first encounter in October of 1931, but Primo had improved since their first fight.

Sharkey came out strong in the early rounds and appeared to easily outbox Primo. Primo kept swinging but was unable to catch Sharkey with any dramatic punches. Along the ropes in the 6th round Primo cut loose with an inside right uppercut that dropped Sharkey to the floor like he had been shot. Sharkey hardly moved while he was counted out. Primo Carnera, nicknamed "the ambling alp" was the new heavyweight champion of the world. People at ringside were surprised at the outcome as Sharkey appeared to be on his way to an easy decision win until he was poleaxed by Primo's uppercut.

The consensus at ringside was that it was a legitimate fight, and in looking at films, I agree that Sharkey was truly knocked out by a powerful right uppercut. Sharkey stated to the day that he died that it was not a fixed fight. Primo returned to Italy as a conquering hero, and he signed to defend his title against old foe Paulino Uzcuden in Rome in October.

Primo had won a controversial decision over Uzcuden in Barcelona in November of 1930, and it figured to be a tough title defense for him. Primo was the aggressor in the fight, and he won nearly every round as he won a legitimate 15-round unanimous decision over the tough Basque. The fight drew a crowd of 70 thousand people.

In March of 1934, Primo returned to the United States to defend his title against former light heavyweight champion Tommy Loughran in Miami, Florida. Primo weighed 270 pounds for this fight to the challengers 184 pounds.

Loughran managed to stay away from Primo's power in the first 10 rounds, but then he faded badly due to the size and strength difference, and Primo walked away with a well-earned 15-round unanimous decision against his smaller opponent.

Primo returned to New York in June of 1934 to take on number one contender Max Baer. Baer had earned his shot at the title by knocking out former heavyweight champion Max Schmeling in 10 rounds in June of 1933. Primo was caught in the first round by one of Baer's wild punches and went down. Primo would go down 2 more times before the round's end. Primo tried to fight back, but he never fully recovered from Baer's first round attack. Primo went down a total of 11 times before the referee stopped the fight in the 11th round. Primo fought on instinct alone after the first round, and was still on his feet when the fight was stopped. Primo had lost his invincibility in the ring after this fight.

In December, Primo returned to the ring and won a 12-round decision over Argentine Victorio Campolo in Buenos Aires, Argentina. In March of 1935, in a battle of the giants, Primo stopped huge Ray Impellitiere in 9 rounds in New York to qualify for a shot at Joe Louis. Primo fought gamely but Louis was too much for him, and he was stopped in the 6th round of their June of 1935 battle. This was to be Primo's last big-time fight as he was stopped twice in 1936 by Leroy Haynes.

During the World War II years, Primo was inactive before returning to the ring in July of 1945 to knock out Michel Blevins. In September, he stopped Sam Gardner in 1 round and then lost 3 fights in a row to Luigi Messina before retiring from the ring in 1946.

Primo's final ring record was 88 wins, and 14 losses. He won 71 fights by knockout. Primo was swindled out of his ring earnings by his corrupt managers and underworld boxing figures. He began a professional wrestling career after retirement from the ring and was a huge success. He wrestled well into the 1960s and became financially secure.

Bud Schulberg's 1956 movie, The Harder They Fall, appeared to be based upon the life story of Primo Carnera. Primo was a man who was brought to the United States as a novelty and was stripped of all his ring earnings by the boxing underworld. He learned to box along the way and was able to win the heavyweight championship of the world. He made two successful defenses of his title, which is two more than Ingemar Johannson made.

Primo is more of a victim then a perpetrator of his fights that were fixed. He should not continue to be punished for the unsavory characters who surrounded his career. He righteously won the heavyweight championship and successfully defended it twice. True, he was no Joe Louis, but he was no Ingemar Johannson either. Primo was inducted into the World Boxing Hall of Fame in 1990, and deserves a plaque in the International Boxing Hall of Fame. Primo died quietly at the age of 60 in his native Sequals, Italy on June 29, 1967.

Gus Lesnevich

Photograph from BoxRec

Chapter 11   *Light Heavyweight*

Gus Lesnevich

Gustav George "Gus" Lesnevich was born on February 22, 1915, in Cliffside Park, New Jersey. Gus was a Golden Gloves champion before he turned professional at the age of 19 in May of 1934. In his professional debut, Gus knocked out Justin Hoffman in 2 rounds.

Fighting as a middleweight, Gus won his first 10 professional fights before he lost a split decision to Jackie Aldare, a fighter who had 80 professional fights. Gus went on a 22-bout win streak until his management made an ill-advised move and put him in the ring in November of 1936 with Middleweight Champion Freddie Steele in a non-title bout. Steele caught Gus cold and knocked him out in the very first round.

After the Steele fight, Gus moved up to the light heavyweight division even though he was only 5 feet 9 inches in height. 1937 was a year of moderate success for Gus as he was stopped by Young Corbett III, but won a 10-round decision over the experienced Alabama Kid. In 1938, Gus defeated former welterweight and middleweight champion Lou Broulliard. In 1939, Gus extended his winning streak by beating the Alabama Kid in a rematch and then defeated former light heavyweight champion Bob Olin.

In November of 1939, Gus received his first title shot when he challenged Light Heavyweight Champion Billy Conn. Gus made a gallant effort, but Conn was a little too fast and elusive in the ring. Conn defeated Gus by unanimous decision.

On New Year's Day in 1940, Gus tuned up for a rematch with Conn by winning a 10-round decision over Dave Clark. In June of 1940, Gus challenged Conn again for the light heavyweight title. Conn stayed one step ahead of Gus and won another 15-round decision.

After defeating Gus, Conn gave up the light heavyweight title to compete as a heavyweight and challenge champion Joe Louis. Anton Christoforidis had defeated Melio Bettina in January of 1941 to gain the National Boxing Association light heavyweight title.

In May of 1941, Gus challenged Christoforidis for the title in New York City. Gus finally won the light heavyweight title with a convincing 15-round decision over the champion. In August, Gus unified the light heavyweight title by winning a close 15-round decision over New Yorker Tami Mauriello. Due to the closeness of the fight, Gus gave Mauriello a rematch in November.

Gus continued his dominance over Mauriello by winning a decisive 15-round decision in the rematch. In 1942, Gus lost a couple of 10-round decisions to heavyweights Jimmy Bivins and Bob Pastor before he joined the Coast Guard during the World War II years. Gus's light heavyweight title was frozen during the war years.

Gus was discharged from the military in 1945 and, after several tune up fights, he traveled to England to defend his title against the top challenger Freddie Mills in May of 1946. Gus gave the Englishman a severe beating and stopped him in the 10th round of their title fight.

1947 was the best year of Gus' professional boxing career. In February, he knocked out undefeated contender Billy Fox in 10 rounds in a title defense, and in May he stopped Melio Bettina in the first round. In July, he won a 10-round decision over Tami Mauriello, and then defeated him a fourth time in October by knocking him out in 7 rounds.

Gus was named Fighter of the year by the Ring magazine for 1947 and he also won the prestigious Edward J. Neil award as their fighter of the year. Billy Fox was screaming for a rematch for the title and in March of 1948, the match was made in New York City.

Gus made quick work of Fox in the rematch by knocking him out in the very first round. In July, Gus returned to London, England for a rematch with British contender Freddie Mills. Gus fought a listless fight and he was outpointed over 15 rounds to lose his title in an upset.

In May of 1949, Gus lost a 15-round decision to future light heavyweight champion Joey Maxim. In August, Gus was rewarded with a title fight with Heavyweight Champion Ezzard Charles. Gus was basically over the hill at this point in his career and Charles was in his prime. Charles cut up and stopped Gus in the 7th round, in the last fight of his career.

Gus retired with a final ring record of 61 wins, 14 defeats, and 5 draws. He won 23 fights by knockout. Gus was a light heavyweight champion for 7 years and during those years he made 5 successful defenses of his title.

Upon retirement, Gus was employed in public relations work for a trucking concern and, also, was a referee for professional boxing matches. Gus was inducted into the New Jersey Boxing Hall of Fame in 1969, the Ring Magazine's Boxing Hall of Fame in 1973, and the World Boxing Hall of Fame in 1988.

It is unbelievable that Gus has not been inducted into the International Boxing Hall of Fame. The problem with Gus not being in the Hall of Fame is not due to any shortcomings on his part as a fighter but more to a lack of boxing knowledge by the boxing writers who cast ballots for the Hall of Fame.

I have read some complaints that Gus did not defend his title against top contenders Archie Moore and Ezzard Charles during the 1940s. Gus fought whomever the promoters put in the ring with him and this should not be a reason to keep him out of the Hall of Fame. Gus passed away at the young age of 49 from a heart attack in his hometown of Cliffside Park, New Jersey in 1964.

Rodrigo Valdes

Photograph from BoxRec

Chapter 12   *Middleweight*

Rodrigo Valdes

Julian Jackson was my first choice to be inducted into the International Boxing Hall of Fame, but that omission was corrected in 2018 when the boxing writers realized their mistake and he was finally given his just due. The next fighter who should be inducted was that great Colombian champion, Rodrigo Valdes.

Rodrigo Valdes was born on December 22, 1946, in Cartagena, Colombia. Rodrigo turned professional on October 25, 1963, when he won a 4-round decision over Orlando Pineda. He won his first 8 professional fights until he was stopped by Rudy Escobar in October of 1965.

Rodrigo went undefeated in his next 16 professional fights before traveling to Quito, Ecuador to lose a 10-round home town decision to one, Daniel Guanin, in February of 1969. In August, Rodrigo began fighting in the United States and won a 10-round decision over veteran Peter Cobblah. Rodrigo began fighting in Las Vegas, Nevada and New York City, and won all of his remaining fights by knockout in 1969.

Rodrigo had mixed success in 1970, winning 3 out of 5 fights. His losses were to veterans Pete Toro and Ralph Palladin. By 1971, Rodrigo was traveling back and forth between Colombia and New York City. He knocked out veterans Bobby Cassidy in August, and Doc Holliday in November in New York City. While in New York,

Rodrigo obtained the services of Hall of Fame trainer and manager Gil Clancy.

Under Clancy's guidance Rodrigo won all of his five fights in 1972. He won fights in Barranquilla, Colombia, New York City, and Paris, France. Rodrigo won his first 4 fights in 1973 in impressive fashion and on September 1st he stepped into the ring with top middleweight contender Bennie Briscoe in Noumea, Caledonia. Rodrigo boxed beautifully and mixed in his power shots to keep Briscoe at bay and win a 12-round unanimous decision. Rodrigo became the number one contender for the World Boxing Council middleweight championship after this fight.

The World Boxing Council ordered the lineal middleweight champion Carlos Monzon to defend his title against Rodrigo within a certain period of time. For unknown reasons, Monzon chose to ignore the World Boxing Councils orders, and he was stripped of their version of the middleweight title. In May of 1974, Rodrigo fought a rematch with Bennie Briscoe for the vacant World Boxing Council middleweight championship in Monte Carlo.

Rodrigo started off strong in the title fight and was doing well until he sustained a cut eye in one of the middle rounds. Briscoe started to take control of the fight in the 6th round as Rodrigo appeared to be fading in the fight. In the 7th round, Rodrigo landed a straight right to Briscoe's chin which knocked him down. Briscoe arose before the 10-count in a dazed condition and the referee immediately stopped the fight. Rodrigo was now the World Boxing Council middleweight champion and Briscoe was a knockout victim for the first, and only, time in his career.

Rodrigo made his first title defense against Frenchman Gratien Tonna in Paris, France in November of 1974. Tonna was a powerfully built middleweight who had power in both fists and had a long list of knockout victories to his credit.

Rodrigo out boxed Tonna in the early rounds and actually got the better of him when they exchanged power punches. Rodrigo had Tonna cut and wobbly when the challenger went down from a right hand after a clinch in the 11th round claiming a foul. The referee did not buy Tonna's act and he was counted out while he was lying on the ground trying to win the title by disqualification.

In May of 1975, Rodrigo defended his title against Argentine Ramon Mendez in Cali, Colombia. Rodrigo out boxed Mendez in the one-sided fight, and then put him to sleep in the 8th round in front of his Colombian fans. In August, Rodrigo defended against Californian Rudy Robles in front of a hometown crowd in Cartagena. Robles chose to run and last the distance instead of trying to win the title. Rodrigo chased Robles all over the ring but could not put him away. Robles did mount something of an offense in the late rounds, but it was too little and too late, as Rodrigo took the unanimous 15-round decision

In March of 1976, Rodrigo returned to Paris to defend against French veteran Max Cohen. Rodrigo was at his best in this fight as he destroyed Cohen with powerful right hands on his way to a 4th round knockout victory. In June, a match was finally made with Carlos Monzon to unify the middleweight title in Monte Carlo. A week before the scheduled fight, one of Rodrigo's brothers was killed in a bar fight in Colombia. Rodrigo asked for a postponement of the fight but he was told that it was impossible, and that he had to go through with the fight.

Rodrigo fought well against Monzon, but he was dropped in the 14th round as Monzon came on strong in the late rounds to win a close 15-round decision. The closeness of the fight, and the circumstances that Rodrigo had to deal with before the fight, called for a rematch. The rematch with Monzon was set for July of 1977, in Monte Carlo again.

Rodrigo started off strong and dropped Monzon in the 2nd round with an overhand right to the jaw. Rodrigo was ahead in the fight after 7 rounds, but Monzon proved his greatness by making the necessary adjustments in the ring to come on strong and batter Rodrigo in the late rounds to win another 15-round unanimous decision. This would prove to be the last fight of Monzon's career as he announced his retirement from the ring in August.

Rodrigo was matched with old foe Bennie Briscoe for the vacant world middleweight championship in November, in Campion d' Italia. Briscoe put up a strong challenge with his vicious body punching, but Rodrigo was able to outbox him to win a close but unanimous decision and become the unified middleweight champion of the world.

After 14 years of professional boxing, Rodrigo was finally the world and lineal middleweight champion. Unfortunately, he would only be the world champion for about 5 months before he was challenged for the title by little known Argentine Hugo Corro in April of 1978.

Rodrigo defended against Corro in San Remo, Italy and it appeared as if he just got old over night. Rodrigo could not keep up with Corro's movement and counterpunching and lost a drab 15-round decision in somewhat of an upset. Corro gave Rodrigo a rematch in Buenos Aires, Argentina in November.

Rodrigo looked even worse in the rematch as he was lucky to last the distance in losing another 15-round decision to Corro. Rodrigo was inactive in 1979 and returned to the ring in 1980. Rodrigo wished to retire as a winner, and he knocked out Charles Hayward in 7 rounds in May and Alberto Almonte in 1 round in November. Both of these fights took place in Bogota, Colombia. Rodrigo realized that he had lost his world class skills and retired after the Almonte fight.

Rodrigo's final ring record was 63 wins, 8 losses, and 2 draws. He won 43 fights by knockout. The Ring magazine included Rodrigo in their list of the 100 greatest punchers of all time. Along with Antonio Cervantes, he is considered one of the greatest fighters to ever come out of Colombia.

Muhammad Ali needed Joe Frazier to push him to greatness, as Stanley Ketchel did with Billy Papke. It could also be said that Carlos Monzon needed to fight Rodrigo to push him to the level of greatness that he obtained in the ring. Clearly if Monzon had not been fighting in the 1970's, Rodrigo would have been the premier middleweight of the decade.

In 2004, while visiting Cartagena, Colombia I had an occasion to talk to Rodrigo at his home near the airport. I mentioned to a local taxi driver that I was a fight fan and knew that Rodrigo lived in Cartagena. The taxi driver advised me that Rodrigo's house was always open to his fight fans and I was driven to his home near the airport. I was met at the front door by this great fighter and he invited me into his home. He showed me all of his boxing trophies, including his World Boxing Council title belt hanging on his living room wall.

We talked about all of his great fights and the fighters he entered the ring with. Rodrigo told me that the hardest puncher he ever faced was Bennie Briscoe. He claimed that Briscoe punched so hard to the body that he felt like quitting in their second fight.

Rodrigo said that the greatest fighter that he ever fought was Carlos Monzon. He said that Monzon was an intelligent fighter who could make adjustments to his style in the ring to defeat an opponent. He made no excuses about his losses to Monzon and stated that he always did the best that he could in all of his fights.

Rodrigo said that when he fought Hugo Corro, he was past his prime and that his legs were gone. He simply said that he could not catch up to Corro and that is when he knew that it was time to quit. He wished to quit a winner and had two fights in 1980 that he won by knockout.

Rodrigo was suffering from diabetes at the time of my visit, and he told me that he had no regrets about his boxing career, and that he owed a lot of his success to the help he received from Gil Clancy and former welterweight and middleweight champion Emile Griffith.

Rodrigo deserves to have his plaque in the International Boxing Hall of Fame. He was a world class boxer and human being. Sadly, I read where he passed away in 2017 at the age of 70 due to a heart attack. May the great boxer rest in peace.

Tippy Larkin

Photograph from BoxRec

Chapter 13   *Welterweight*

Tippy Larkin

Tippy Larkin was born Antonio (Tony) Pilleteri on November 11, 1917, in Garfield, New Jersey. Antonio immediately Americanized his ring name to Tippy Larkin before he turned professional. He used Tippy from the initials in his first name and used his brothers last boxing name to come up with his ring name. Tippy, at 5 feet 7 inches in height, boxed as a small welterweight and he was nicknamed the "Garfield Gunnar".

At the age of 17, Tippy entered the Civilian Conservation Core in 1934 and started boxing as an amateur. He quickly compiled an unsubstantiated record of 9 straight knockout wins.

Tippy turned professional in 1935 with a 3-round loss to Ed McGillick. Tippy won his next 17 fights before losing a decision to Johnny Schibelli in June of 1936. In 1936 alone, Tippy fought an incredible 26 times with only 2 losses. In 1937, Tippy began fighting 10-round matches and won 12 of 13 fights, losing only to Micky Duca. Tippy also defeated future welterweight champion Freddie (Red) Cochrane 3 times.

In 1938, Tippy won all 14 of his matches including 2 more wins over Freddie (Red) Cochrane. Tippy also defeated Mickey Duca in a rematch. In 1939, Tippy won 7 of 9 matches. He lost a close decision to former super lightweight champion Jackie (Kid) Berg, and was shockingly knocked out by Al "Bummy" Davis in 5 rounds.

The Davis fight was the first sign that Tippy had a chink in his armor as it would be the first of his 10 career losses by knockout.

In March of 1940, he was stopped in 1 round by future lightweight champion Lew Jenkins. This proved that even though Tippy was a beautiful well-schooled boxer, his chin could be reached by a knockout puncher like Jenkins.

Tippy rebounded by winning his 4 remaining fights in 1940 and he won all 9 of his fights in 1941. Tippy won his first 10 fights in 1942 and then fought Beau Jack for the New York State Athletic Commissions lightweight title. Tippy boxed well in the first 2 rounds but Jack reached his chin in the 3rd round to win by a technical knockout.

Tippy took on 3-division returning champion Henry Armstrong in March of 1943. Armstrong could hardly lay a glove on Tippy in the first round, but Armstrong caught up to him in the 2nd round and stopped him. Tippy won his next 13 fights in 1943 to finally climb atop the world welterweight rankings.

In January of 1944, Tippy fought to a draw with Bobby Ruffin, and then defeated top contender Allie Stolz in 3 rounds in March at Madison Square Garden in New York. Tippy won all 4 of his fights in 1945, including a 10-round decision over top contender Willie Joyce in New York City.

Tippy won his first 3 fights in 1946 and then he was matched with Willie Joyce in a rematch for the World Junior Welterweight championship in Boston, Massachusetts. Tippy put on a boxing clinic to win a 12-round decision over Joyce and become the world junior welterweight champion. Tippy successfully defended his title by again beating Joyce by a 12-round decision in September, in New York City.

Tippy gave up the junior welterweight championship to campaign for a shot at the world welterweight championship. In February of 1947, Tippy's weak chin was exposed again as welterweight contender Charley Fusari stopped him in 9 rounds in New York City.

In March of 1947, Tippy fought probably the best fight of his career when he out boxed another master boxer in Billy Graham at Madison Square Garden. Tippy pitched a near shutout to win a 10-round decision over the top-rated Graham. Tippy won 5 of his 6 fights in 1947 losing only to World Lightweight Champion Ike Williams in a non-title bout.

In 1948, Tippy won 7 of 8 matches losing only to Charley Fusari again by knockout. In 1949, Tippy won 6 of 7 matches, losing only to upcoming welterweight contender Bernard Docusen by knockout. Tippy took a year off from boxing in 1950 and returned in 1951 to win all 3 of his fights by 8-round decisions.

In 1952, Tippy won 2 of 4 fights and retired after being knocked out by Steve Marcello in December. Tippy's final ring record was an incredible 131 wins, 13 losses and 1 draw. He won 58 fights by knockout and was stopped 10 times in his career.

Tippy passed away on December 10th, 1991, at the age of 74. He was one of the best pure boxers of all time. He lost only to the top tier fighters of his day who had a knockout punch. Tippy was inducted into the World Boxing Hall of Fame in 1992

Tippy should receive strong consideration for induction into the International Boxing Hall of Fame due to the fact that he had an amazing record against the best fighters of his day and that he was a former junior welterweight champion of the world.

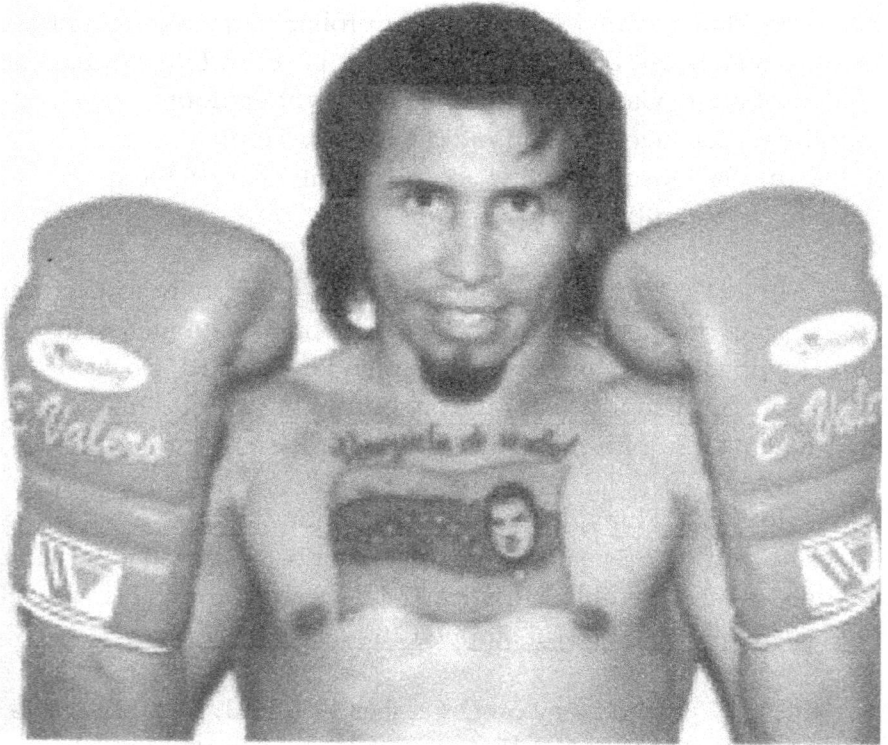

Edwin Valero

Photograph from BoxRec

Chapter 14   *Lightweight*

Edwin Valero

Edwin (El Inca) Valero was born on December 3, 1981, in Merida, Venezuela. Edwin started boxing at the age of 12 and compiled an amateur boxing record of 86 wins and 6 losses. He won 57 amateur bouts by knockout.

Edwin was a Venezuelan National amateur champion as well as a Central and South American amateur boxing champion. In February of 2001, Edwin was involved in a serious motorcycle accident and fractured his skull. A blood clot was surgically removed and he was cleared to turn professional in Venezuela.

As a professional, Edwin was an instant success as he started off his career with 18 first round knockouts. He had incredible power in both fists and it appeared that all he had to do was to touch an opponent with his incredible power and they were unable to continue the fight. In his 19th professional fight he had to go 2 rounds for the first time to knockout Genaro Trazancos in March of 2006.

In August of 2006, Edwin traveled to Panama City to challenge Panamanian champion Vicente Mosquera for the World Boxing Association super featherweight title. Edwin came out fast and dropped Mosquera twice in the first round. Mosquera fought back hard and dropped Edwin in the 3rd round. Edwin showed that he had stamina to go along with his punching power as he wore Mosquera down for a 10th round technical knockout victory.

2007 would turn out to be a busy year for Edwin as he stopped Michael Lozada in the first round in January and Nobuhito Honmo in 8 rounds in May. In December, Edwin stopped Zaid Zavaleta in 3 rounds. All of his knockout victories occurred in title defenses.

In June of 2008, Edwub stopped Takehiro Shimada in 7 rounds in Tokyo, Japan for the 4th defense of his super featherweight title. Edwin was having trouble making the 130-pound super featherweight limit and decided to move up to the 135-pound lightweight division.

In April of 2009, Edwin made his United States debut by challenging Antonio Pitalua for the World Boxing Council lightweight title in Austin, Texas. Some ring observers were not sure if Edwin would be as powerful in the lightweight division as he had been in the super featherweight division.

It was obvious that Edwin lost none of his power in his move to the lightweight division as he stopped Pitalua in 2 rounds to gain the lightweight title. In December, Edwin returned to LaGuaira, Venezuela to defend his title against Hector Velazquez. Edwin thoroughly dominated Velazquez before stopping him in the 7th round of his first lightweight title defense.

In February of 2010, Edwin fought the biggest and final bout of his remarkable ring career. He defended his title against number one contender Antonio DeMarco in Monterey, Mexico. DeMarco was a popular contender and he was fighting in front of thousands of his countryman. Hostile crowds never seemed to bother Edwin and the fight was televised on national television in the United States.

Edwin started off in his usual aggressive manner, but in the 2nd round of the fight, he caught an accidental elbow by DeMarco that opened up a horrific cut over his right eye. If the fight were held in the United States, there would have been a good chance that the fight would have gone to the scorecards for a technical decision.

This fight was in Mexico, and it was allowed to continue. Edwin miraculously did not appear to be hampered by the cut as he launched a non-stop whirlwind attack to batter DeMarco from one end of the ring to the other. DeMarco had a strong chin and he hung in the fight until the bell sounded to start the 10th round. The fight was one sided and DeMarco was so badly battered that he could not come off of his stool to continue. Edwin was awarded a 10th round technical knockout victory and even the capacity Mexican crowd cheered him after the fight.

The victory brought Edwin's record to 27 wins and no defeats. He had won all of his fights by knockout. In March of 2010, Edwin vacated his lightweight title and announced he would continue his ring career in the 140-pound super lightweight division. Unfortunately, like Carlos Monzon before him, Edwin was unable to control his temper outside of the ring. Shortly after Edwin vacated his title, he was accused of assaulting his wife, however the charges were eventually dropped.

In April of 2010, Edwin's wife Jennifer Carolina Valero was found dead in a hotel room in Valencia, Carabobo, Venezuela. Edwin was arrested for his wife's murder and taken into custody. The day after his arrest, he committed suicide by hanging in his jail cell.

There is no doubt that the name Valero is still toxic to some voting members of boxing's Hall of Fame. As far as ring records are concerned, he had an absolutely perfect record as he was a two time world champion and he defeated the best fighters in two weight divisions.

In some sports, his reputation would permanently bar him from the Hall of Fame. However, his sport was boxing, and if history repeats itself, he will probably be inducted sometime in the near future. He has precedent on his side, as middleweight champion Billy Papke was inducted into the International Boxing Hall of Fame after murdering his wife in 1936, as well as middleweight champion Carlos Monzon, who murdered his wife in 1988.

Davey Moore

Photograph from BoxRec

Chapter 15 *Featherweight*

Davey Moore

Davey Moore, aka The Springfield Rifle, was born on November 1, 1933, in Lexington, Kentucky. Davey moved to Springfield, Ohio with his family and took up amateur boxing. In 1952, he won the National Amateur Athletic Union bantamweight championship and represented the United States in the 1952 Olympic games held in held in Helsinki. Davey was eliminated in the 3rd round of bouts held in the bantamweight division.

After completing his amateur career, Davey turned professional on May 11, 1953, with 6-round decision over Willie Reece. Davey won his first 6 matches until he lost a 6-round decision to Russell Tague in October.

Davey won his next 3 fights, and then lost a 10-round decision to Jackie Blair in February of 1954. More victories followed with Davey winning the Ohio State featherweight title with a 9th round technical knockout victory over Eddie Burgin in 9 rounds in December of 1954.

In 1955, Davey fought in Havana, Cuba, in Colon, Panama, and in El Paso, Texas winning some main event bouts and losing others. Davey won 2 out of 3 fights in 1956, and really hit his stride in 1957 with wins over featherweight contenders Gil Cadilli and Isidro Martinez.

In 1958, Davey moved his base of operations to Los Angeles, California and became known as "the Mexican killer" for defeating the likes of Vince Delgado, Lauro Salas, and Kid Anahuac. A one round knockout of power punching Mexican Ricardo Moreno in December of 1958 earned Davey a shot at the world featherweight title.

In March of 1959, Davey challenged Nigerian champion Hogan (Kid) Bassey for the featherweight title in Los Angeles. Davey out jabbed and peppered Bassey with left hooks and right hands until the champion quit in the 13th round. After boxing 6 years as a professional all over the world, Davey had finally become a world champion.

At 5 foot 3 inches in height, Davey was short for a featherweight but he had an excellent jab, devastating left hook, and lethal right cross. He could box well and had power in both fists. Davey had been well schooled as an amateur boxer.

The rematch with Bassey was set for August of 1959. Davey made quicker work of Bassey in the rematch, stopping him in the 11th round of the title fight. Davey just proved to be too quick and powerful for the ex-Nigerian champion. Davey had become a fan favorite in Los Angeles, with George Parnassus as his promoter and Willie Ketchum as his manager.

After his second title defense, Davey went to London in October to knock out Bobby Neill in one round, and win a 10-round decision over Hilario Morales in San Francisco in December in non-title fights.

Davey went on a tour of Venezuela in 1960 and, surprisingly, was stopped in 7 rounds by power punching Carlos Hernandez in March in Caracas. Davey regrouped in August when he traveled to Japan to win a 15-round decision over Japanese challenger Kazuo Takayama in a featherweight title defense.

Davey opened 1961 with non-title wins in Paris, France and Madrid, Spain before defending his title against Danny Valdez in August. Davey came out at the first bell swinging, and he stopped Valdez cold in the very first round for his 3rd successful title defense. Davey defeated contenders Gil Cadilli, and Pelon Cervantes in non-title matches before he flew back to Tokyo to give Kazuo Takayama a rematch for the title in November. Takayama lasted the distance again, but Davey was dominant in defending his title with a 15-round decision over the stubborn challenger.

In March of 1962, Davey stopped Cisco Andrade in 7 rounds in Los Angeles, and Mario Diaz in 2 rounds in July. In August, Davey flew to Helsinki, Finland to defend his title against contender Olli Maki. The trip was somewhat of a 10 year homecoming anniversary for Davey as he had fought in the Olympics in Helsinki in 1952. Davey made quick work of Maki, blasting him out in the 2nd round for his 5th successful title defense.

In February of 1963, Davey stopped Gil Cadilli in 5 rounds of a rematch held in San Jose, California, before defending his title against top ranked Cuban contender Ultiminio (Sugar) Ramos. Davey defended his title against Ramos as part of a big boxing extravaganza at Dodger Stadium in Los Angeles in March of 1963.

The fight was close and vicious from the start with Ramos leading slightly at the end of 9 rounds. Davey was floored in the 10th round and the back of his head snapped against the bottom rope on the way down. Davey got up and the bell rang as he was being pummeled against the ropes. Davey did not come out for the 11th round, and he collapsed later back in his dressing room. He was taken to a hospital where he lapsed into a coma and died several days after the fight.

After Davey Moore's death there was an outcry to abolish boxing as Benny (Kid) Paret and Alejandro Lavorante also died from boxing related injuries during this same time period. The State of

California even talked about abolishing boxing for a short period of time. Musician Bob Dylan even wrote a song about Davey's death in the ring.

President John F. Kennedy was shot and killed later during the year and a nation turned away from the abolishment of boxing to national mourning of the Presidents death. Davey's final ring record was 59 wins, 7 losses, and 1 draw. He won 30 fights by knockout.

In 2013, to commemorate the 50th anniversary of Davey's death, the city of Springfield, Ohio erected an 8-foot statute of him in a park near where he grew up. Even his old foe Sugar Ramos showed up for the unveiling of the statute. Davey Moore should be remembered for a lot more than just his tragic last fight which ended in his death, and the clamoring for the abolishment of boxing. Davey was a solid ring man who was a world champion who made 5 successful defenses of his world title.

It's too bad, as of this date, that the International Boxing Hall of Fame has forgotten about Davey and not put his plaque up in Canastota where it belongs.

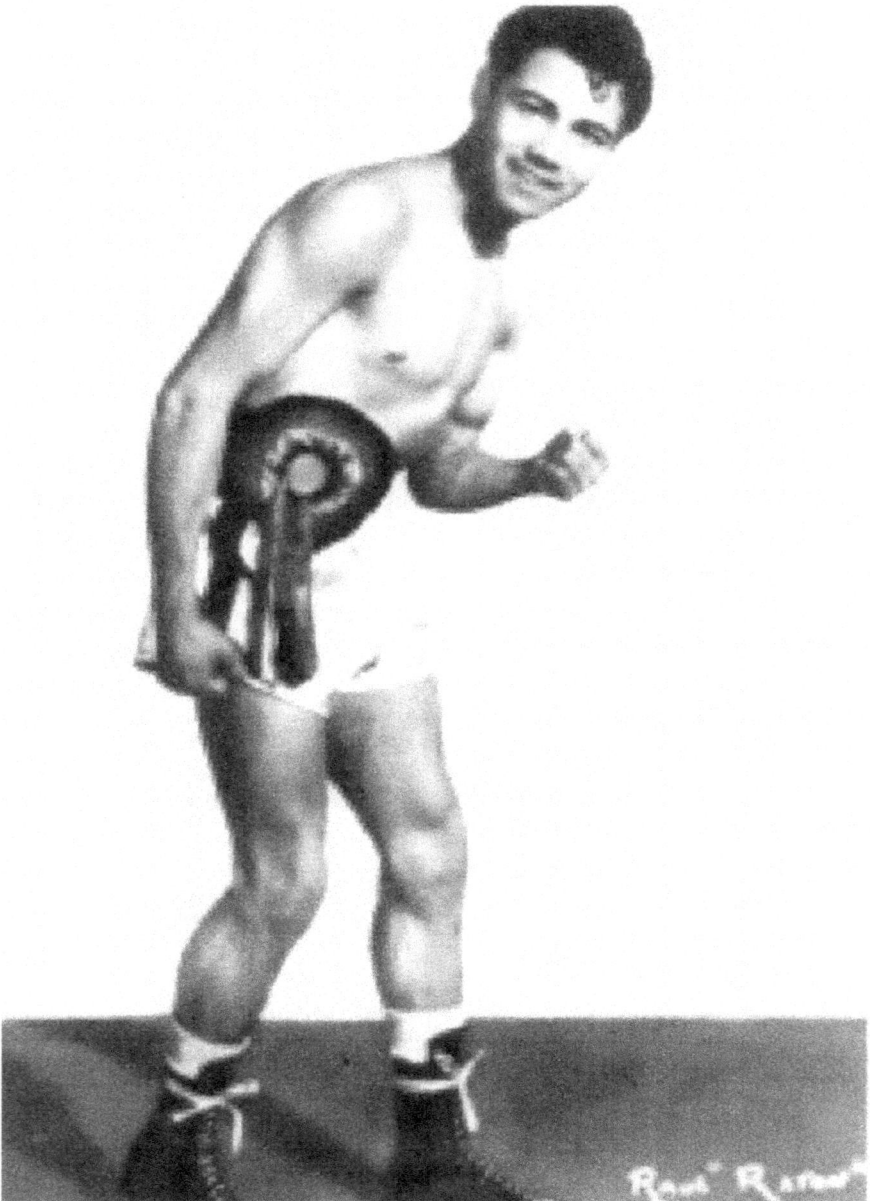

Raul (Raton) Macias

Photograph from BoxRec

Chapter 16   *Bantamweight*

Raul (Raton) Macias

Raul Macias was born on July 28, 1934, in Teptio, Distrito Federal, Mexico. Raul began his amateur boxing career at age 14 and was a bronze medal winner in the 1951 Pan American games. He also represented Mexico as a bantamweight in the 1952 Olympic Games in Helsinki, Finland. Raul lost his second bout in the Olympics.

Raul turned professional in November of 1952, and won 2 decisions over Chucho Tello during the month. In April of 1953, Raul was already fighting and winning 10-round fights, and in October he won a 12-round decision over Beto Couary for the Mexican Bantamweight title.

In January of 1954, Raul won a 10-round decision over Alberto Reyes, and in March he stopped power punching bantamweight contender Billy Peacock in 7 rounds in front of his hometown fans in Mexico City.

Raul returned to the ring the following month and defended his Mexican bantamweight title by winning a 12-round unanimous decision over Fili Nava. In September. Raul fought 1952 Olympic flyweight gold medal winner Nate Brooks for the North American bantamweight championship in Mexico City.

Before 50 thousand fans, Raul won a 12-round unanimous decision to become the top contender for the world bantamweight title. Raul challenged Thailand's Chamroen Songkitrat for the vacant National Boxing Association bantamweight title in in March of 1955 at the Cow Palace in San Francisco, California.

Raul started off boxing well and hurting his opponent with left hooks to the head. Raul dropped Songkitrat twice in the 6th round, but his durable opponent fought back gamely until dropped twice more, and stopped in the 11th round. In a little over 2 years of fighting as a professional, Raul had made it to the top of the bantamweight division. Raul was very charismatic and he became what could be regarded as the "first great Mexican idol".

Raul ran his record up to 19 wins and no defeats with a couple of non-title wins before facing Billy Peacock in a rematch in June of 1955 at the famed Olympic auditorium in Los Angeles, California. Raul had knocked out Peacock in their first fight, and he was a big favorite to triumph again in the rematch.

Raul started off strong and was exchanging left hooks with Peacock near a neutral corner, when he caught a left hook that broke his jaw and dropped him to the canvas for the 10-count. The auditorium when silent as the stunned Mexican fans could not believe their eyes, that their hero had actually been defeated. Raul had to be hospitalized after the fight for treatment for his broken jaw.

Raul returned to the ring in October and looked lackadaisical in winning a sloppy 10-round decision over one Cecil Schoonmaker in Corpus Christi, Texas. Raul eventually returned to form and reeled off 4 straight non-title knock out victories before he defended his title against Filipino Leo Espinosa in March of 1956 in Mexico City.

Raul had returned to championship form as he demolished Espinosa inside of 10 rounds for another knockout victory. Mexican fight fans could not believe that this was the same fighter who had been stopped by Billy Peacock up north in Los Angeles in 1955.

Raul reeled off 9 straight victories, with 8 wins coming by knockout, before he defended his title for the second time against another Filipino fighter named Dommy Ursua, in June of 1957 at San Francisco's Cow Palace. Raul paced himself well during the fight and had cut his opponent around the eyes in the 6th round. Raul kept up his two-fisted attack until he finally stopped Ursua with combinations in the 11th round of the title fight.

In September, Raul tuned up for his third title defense when he knocked out Panchito Gonzalez in 5 rounds in Juarez, Mexico. In November, Raul took on French-Algerian bantamweight Alphonse Halimi for the unified world bantamweight title.

Halimi was a power puncher who could match Raul's speed, and the first 3 rounds were close until Raul was shaken by a hook to the jaw in the 4th round. Halimi maintained an early lead but Raul fought back hard to keep the fight close. Raul closed strongly in the 15th and final round, but Halimi matched him punch for punch until the final bell. Many in the crowd felt that Raul's strong finish earned him a close decision but the judges thought otherwise when they awarded Halimi a split decision victory.

Raul would never get a chance to fight for another title. In November, he returned to the ring to win a 10-round decision over Kid Irapuato in Tijuana, Mexico, and he won all 3 of his fights in 1959. Raul took a 3 year break from the ring, and returned for one final fight when he knocked out Chocolate Zambrano in 5 rounds in October of 1962 in Guadalajara, Mexico.

Raul retired after the Zambrano fight in 1962 with a final ring record of 41 wins and just 2 losses. He won 25 fights by knockout. After retirement, Raul trained fighters, and became a popular figure in the Mexican film industry. Raul was always in demand for public appearances right up until his death at the age of 74 on March 23, 2009.

Raul has been inducted into the World Boxing Hall of Fame, and I am not really sure why he has not been considered for entry into the International Boxing Hall of Fame. His outstanding ring record and popularity to this day in his native Mexico should make him a strong candidate for entry into the Hall.

Betulio Gonzalez

Photograph from BoxRec

Chapter 17   *Flyweight*

Betulio Gonzalez

Betulio Segundo Gonzalez was born on October 24, 1949, in Maracaibo, Venezuela. Betulio and Miguel Canto of Mexico were considered to be the premier boxers in the flyweight division during the decade of the 1970's. Betulio is still considered to this day to be the best fighter to ever come out of Venezuela and is regarded as a national hero in his country.

Betulio turned professional on April 24, 1968, with a knockout over Elio Monzant, and then won his first 10 fights easily before he fought a draw with Jose Brizuela. Betulia defeated Brizuela in a rematch, and then knocked out Hector Criollo for the Venezuelan flyweight title on October 10th, of 1969.

Betulio suffered his first defeat on a fluke knockout blow delivered by Felix Marquez on March 6, 1970. Marquez shocked the odds makers as he was fighting in just his second professional fight. Betulio defeated Marquez in a rematch while defending his Venezuelan flyweight title, and also defeated world ranked Ignacio Espinal and Bernabe Villacampo to set the stage for his first attempt at a world title.

In April of 1971, Betulio traveled to Japan to challenge ill-fated champion Masao Ohba for the World Boxing Association flyweight title. Ohba was too clever and experienced for Betulio, and he walked away with a 15-round unanimous decision victory.

Not to be discouraged Betulio won 3 straight fights and then challenged World Boxing Council Flyweight Champion Erbito Salavarria in Caracas, Venezuela. Betulio's second attempt at a title ended in a disputed draw. Allegations were made by the local boxing commission that Salavarria used an illegal stimulant during the fight, and the World Boxing Council declared the title vacant.

On June 3, 1972, Betulio won his first world title when he knocked out Socrates Batoto in 4 rounds in Caracas, Venezuela for the vacant title. Betulio immediately lost the title to Venice Borkhorsor by knockout in September in Bangkok, Thailand.

As usual, Betulio persevered and went on a 4-bout winning streak before he defeated the legendary Miguel Canto by majority decision in Maracaibo, Venezuela in August of 1973 to claim the World Boxing Association flyweight title for the second time. Betulio used his aggressiveness and non-stop punching to take his second title.

Betulio stopped Alberto Morales in 11 rounds in November of 1973, and knocked out Franco Udella in 10 rounds in July of 1974 in successful title defenses. Udella had been moving up from the junior flyweight division and was no match for Betulio's power.

In October of 1974, Betulio traveled to Japan and lost his title to Shoji Oguma by decision. In 1975, and in 1976, Betulio lost decisions to Miguel Canto in attempts at Canto's flyweight title. After an 8 fight winning streak, Betulio challenged Guty Espadas senior for the World Boxing Association flyweight title in Maracay, Venezuela in August of 1978. Betulio won a 15-round decision over Espadas to claim his third world flyweight title.

Betulio fought one of the best fights of his career when he stopped Chilean challenger Martin Vargas in 12 rounds in November, to defend his world title. Betulio retained his title when his fight with Shoji Oguma was declared a draw in 15 rounds of fighting in Japan in January of 1979. In a rematch in July, Betulio knocked out his stubborn Japanese challenger in 12 rounds in another successful title defense.

Betulio would lose his flyweight title for the final time when Luis Ibarra surprisingly defeated him by a 15-round decision. In 1981, Betulio challenged Juan Herrera for the flyweight championship and was stopped in 7 rounds. Betulio lost his last bid for a world title when he lost a split decision to Argentine boxer Santo Laciar in Maracaibo, Venezuela.

Betulio retired from the ring after losing to Rodolfo Blanco by knockout in 1988 just prior to the mandatory boxer retirement age of 40 in Venezuela. In 20 years of boxing, Betulio's final ring record was 76 wins, 12 defeats, and 4 draws. He won 52 fights by knockout. As stated previously, Betulio is a national hero in Venezuela, and is considered by many that he was the greatest boxer that Venezuela ever produced. Then the question is why this 3-time world champion during the 1970's is not in boxing's hall of fame?

Certainly, he has all the proper credentials for entry in the Hall. Many boxing writers from the United States vote for entrants and, surely, Venezuela is not a popular country in the United States. I don't believe the answer should lie in the country that he is from though.

I believe the answer lies in the ignorance of the boxing writers who cast ballots for entry into the Hall of Fame. The writers do well if the fighter is famous or recently retired. If the boxer has been retired for over 30 years, then he gets lost in the balloting shuffle. The exclusion of Gonzalez from the Hall of Fame is another indication that the balloting for the Hall of Fame is seriously flawed.

Charlie (Devil) Green with Malcolm (Flash) Gordon

Photograph from IBRO Journal, Issue 132, December 2016

Special Categories and Considerations

Chapter 18   Jimmy Cannon Writer's Award

Malcolm (Flash) Gordon

Malcolm (Flash) Gordon was a muckraking little writer from New York City who published "Tonight's Boxing Program" from the 1960's to the mid 1980's. It is believed that Gordon was born around 1947, and, in appearance, he was described as looking like Woody Allen. He has been described by other journalists as an unrepentant non-conformist of the first order. It is extremely difficult to this day to find any photos of the little writer.

He lived in Sunnyside Queens in New York for the past 50 years of his life in a one bedroom apartment where he would crank out his Tonight's Boxing Program and sell them at boxing matches at Madison Square Garden, and in other small clubs in Northern New Jersey, and in Manhattan. I personally subscribed to his newsletter during the late 1970's and early 1980's.

He came out with worldwide boxing results ahead of the monthly boxing magazines and the amount of fight results he listed worldwide was absolutely amazing in the pre-internet days. He was able to do all of this by buying up all the newspapers he could find with fight results and then publish the results with an offset machine in his apartment.

Gordon took on anyone and everyone in his boxing newsletter who he felt was a negative force in boxing. He took on Ring Magazine, Don King, boxing promoter Ben Greene, and, what he called, the alphabet boys (World Boxing Association, World Boxing Council, International Boxing Federation, and World Boxing Organization). I don't know what it means, but many of the people that he attacked like Don King and Bob Arum, are currently in Boxing's Hall of Fame. His nick name for boxing publisher Nat Fleischer was Nat Fossil for his outdated boxing records, he called Bob Arum 'Massa Bob', for his dealings with apartheid South African promotors and fighters, and his name for Don King was Dung King for just about everything he was involved in.

Gordon's biggest claim to fame was his exposure of a United States boxing tournament sponsored by Don King, the Ring Magazine, and televised by ABC television. Gordon noticed that the fighter's records in the tournament were inaccurate and falsified, and brought this to the attention of ABC television officials and even wrote letters to United States Senators.

The tournament was eventually cancelled by ABC television, and Gordon received a lot of the credit for exposing the boxing scam to the general public. In the early 1980's, a promoter named Harold Smith paid a fee to use Muhammad Ali's name to form a promotional company called Muhammad Ali Professional Sports (MAPS) to promote boxing. Smith paid fighters huge sums of money to promote fights.

It turned out that Smith and a Wells Fargo bank insider had used an elaborate scheme to bilk the bank out of over 21 million dollars in funds that Smith used to promote fights and pay his fighters. Smith was sentenced to 10 years in prison, and Gordon was gaining a reputation as a boxing crusader. Though this did nothing to help Muhammad Ali's reputation, the fighter himself was never connected to this scam.

In the mid-1980's, Gordon was working on a North American ring record book when he just seemed to disappear. Some people claimed that the book was just too much for him to complete, but for whatever reason, he was not heard from for about 30 years until the news came out that he had died in 2015. Apparently, he had been living in his same little apartment in Sunnyside at the time of his death. It was also reported that he died a pauper and had to be buried in a cemetery for indigents in New York.

Gordon was an idealist of the first order. I am sure if he was inducted into the International Boxing Hall of Fame, he would refuse the honor of induction and would not wish to stand next to the people he wrote about like Don King or Bob Arum.

From the 1960's thru the 1980's Gordon brought a sort of integrity and idealism to the sport of boxing. Though he would refuse the honor, the International Boxing Hall of Fame should find a place for this little influential icon of boxing journalism.

Senator Carey Estes Kefauver

Photograph from en.wikipedia.org

Chapter 19   Boxing's Clean Up Award

Kefauver Committee

Carey Estes Kefauver was a Democratic Senator from Tennessee who was born on July 26, 1903. Okay, so now you are wondering what is his name doing in a boxing book? Well, old Estes just happened to chair a committee that helped to break the stranglehold that mobsters and James D. Norris, head of the International Boxing Club (IBC), had on boxing from the end of World War II until, roughly, 1960.

Beginning in 1950, Senator Kefauver chaired a special Senate committee appointed to investigate organized crime. The hearings were televised nationally, and those few people who owned television sets got to see what gangsters and Mafioso's really looked like.

By 1960, Senator Kefauver was well known in national political circles and, in 1956, he ran on the Democratic ticket as a vice presidential nominee in a losing effort to the Republicans, and President Dwight D. Eisenhower. 1960 was also the year when Kefauver and his committee turned their attention to organized crime in boxing.

During the Senate hearings, it was revealed that the International Boxing Club operated out of Chicago by President James D. Norris had ties to mobsters Frank "Blinky Palermo and

Frankie Carbo. The International Boxing Club also had a foothold in New York and, if a boxer was not managed or promoted by the mobsters or the International Boxing Club, he could not hope to get a title fight or make any real money in the sport.

Palermo and Carbo received prison sentences for extortion, racketeering, and conspiracy. Carbo received 25 years, and Palermo 15 years in prison. Even though the multi-millionaire Norris escaped a prison sentence, The International Boxing Club was deemed a monopoly, and the courts ordered its dissolution.

Truman Gibson, the attorney for the mobsters and The International Boxing Club, received 5 years' probation for his part in the monopoly. The real victims were the professional fighters who should have made millions of dollars, such as ex-lightweight champion Ike Williams, who ended up broke and blind to show for all his years in the ring. Ex-middleweight champion Jake (The Raging Bull) LaMotta had to throw a fight in 1947 to mob-controlled boxer Billy Fox, to eventually even get to fight for the middleweight title in 1949.

Some sportswriters like one of my favorites, Jimmy Cannon, called boxing "the red light district of sports" and spoke out against the mob control, but many writers of the day were bought off and chose to look the other way rather to report the facts. Some fights in the 1950's were so obviously fixed, that even the general public was aware that something was amiss. Ex-welterweight champion Johnny Saxton was a mob controlled fighter and his decisions wins over Kid Gavilan and Carmen Basilio in the 1950s were absolutely scandalous. In the end 1950's, welterweight champions, Saxton, and Johnny Bratton, ended up broke and in mental institutions.

It took surprise welterweight champion Don Jordan, and his management team, to refuse to go along with the mob to start the flow of evidence against the International Boxing Club, and the mobsters. Senator Kefauver is an unlikely candidate for the

International Boxing Hall of Fame, but it took this 'nerd' of a Senator from Tennessee to help clean up boxing of the filth involved in the sport. Some of Senator Kefauver's ideas of Federal control over boxing never materialized but, in the end, he owed nothing to boxing, but boxing owed a great deal to this thoroughly decent and trustworthy human being.

Boxing to this day is not without its scandalous decisions especially in Las Vegas. Manny Pacquaio has been victimized in fights in Australia and in Las Vegas. Is there anyone out there who did not think that Canelo Alveraz actually lost his first fight with Gennady Golovkin? On a lesser note, did Deontay Wilder really deserve a draw against Englishman Tyson Fury, even though he was out boxed for most of the fight? Recently Jermell Charlo won 9 out of 12 rounds defending his super welterweight title against Tony Harrison. The judges voted unanimously for Harrison in one of the worst miscarriages of justice seen on television in a long time.

Actually, even though Mixed Martial Arts fights are only from 3 to 5 rounds, their decisions seem to be more just then professional boxing. So, does boxing need Federal Control? I don't think so, but I would settle for Malcolm (Flash) Gordon, and Estes Kefauver enshrined in the special categories section of the International Boxing Hall of Fame.

Carlos Monzon

Photograph from fightgameblog.com

Chapter 20   Fighter of the Decade

Carlos Monzon

Picking the fighter of the decade was a difficult choice. The choice was between Muhammad Ali, Roberto Duran, and Carlos Monzon. Of the three only, Carlos Monzon was unbeaten throughout the decade.

Ali won the heavyweight title twice during the decade. The first time was in 1974 when he stopped George Foreman in Zaire, and the second time was when he won his rematch with Leon Spinks in 1978. During the decade Ali suffered defeats to Joe Frazier, Ken Norton, and Leon Spinks. It could probably be said that Ali was in his prime in the 1960's when he first won the title in 1964 from Sonny Liston, until he was stripped of the title in 1967.

A strong case could be made for Roberto Duran as the fighter of the decade as he only suffered one defeat during the decade, and that was to Esteban DeJesus in their first non-title fight in 1972, in New York City. Duran would go on the defeat DeJesus in their rematch, and in the third rubber match between the two. Duran successfully defended his lightweight title 12 times during the decade.

Monzon was absolutely perfect during the decade of the 1970's as he won all 15 world title fights that he was involved in. He won the middleweight title from Nino Benvenuti in 1970, and defended it successfully 14 times before he retired in 1977. As previously stated, Monzon would not taste defeat during the entire decade. In fact, only a couple of his fights were even close.

Monzon dominated the middleweight division like no other middleweight champion before him, and by splitting hairs, I chose Monzon over Duran as the fighter of the decade.

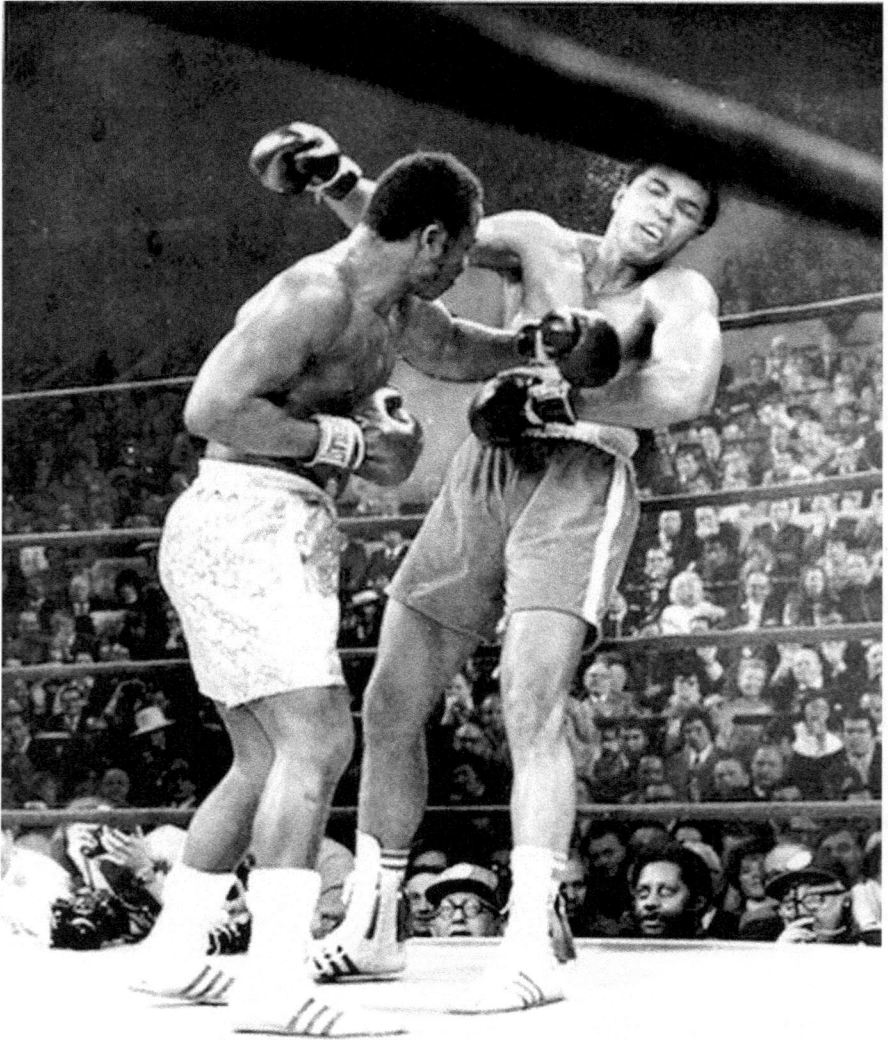

Joe Frazier and Muhammad Ali

Photograph from gettyimages.co.uk

Chapter 21   *Fight of the Decade*

Muhammad Ali vs. Joe Frazier 1, 1971

There is no doubt that there many great fights during the decade of the 1970's but, in my mind, the two greatest fights were Muhammad Ali vs. Joe Frazier 1 in 1971, in New York City, and Muhammad Ali vs. Joe Frazier 3 in Manila in 1975

Of the two fights I believe that Ali vs. Frazier 1 on March 8, 1971 at Madison Square Garden had the most historical value. Ali v. Frazier 1 in 1971 was labeled "The Fight of the Century" by the news media and the boxing public. The fight definitely lived up to its great expectations.

Ali had not fought from the time he was stripped of his heavyweight title in 1967 until his first comeback fight with Jerry Quarry in October of 1970. He stopped Quarry in 3 rounds, and then stopped Oscar (Ringo) Bonavena in 15 rounds in December to set up the title fight with Joe Frazier in March of 1971.

Ali's anti-Vietnam war stance was shared by many Americans and he became a sort of cult figure lecturing on college campuses across the nation during his exile from boxing. While Ali was away from boxing the World Boxing Association held a tournament to find a successor to the heavyweight throne. Ali's former sparring partner, Jimmy Ellis, defeated Jerry Quarry in the final bout of the tournament to claim the vacant World Boxing Association heavyweight title in April of 1968.

Joe Frazier, who had won the Olympic gold medal in the heavyweight division of the 1964 Olympics, elected not to participate in the tournament, and he stopped Buster Mathis in Madison Square Garden in March of 1968 to gain New York recognition as world heavyweight champion. Frazier and Jimmy Ellis would eventually meet in a title unification match in February of 1970. Frazier would stop Ellis in 5 rounds to become world champion, while Ali was still largely recognized as the lineal champion.

The upcoming fight between Ali and Frazier was entitled "The Fight of the Century" and it was scheduled for March 8, 1971, in Madison Square Garden. Each fighter was guaranteed 2.5 million dollars, which was a huge sum of money in 1971.

Ali claimed that he was the peoples champion and tried to paint Joe Frazier as an "Uncle Tom" and a fighter representing the white establishment. Ali also taunted Frazier by taunting him and saying that he looked like a gorilla.

Both fighters were undefeated going into the contest. Frazier was undefeated in 26 professional fights and Ali had been undefeated in 31 professional fights. To many fight fans, Ali was considered the lineal heavyweight champion as he had never lost his title inside the ring.

Ali weighed in at 215 pounds for the fight, and Frazier came in at 205 ½ pounds. Frazier was the slight favorite at fight time, due to the fact that he had been the more active fighter in the recent years leading up to the fight.

As previously stated, Ali, the challenger, entered the ring wearing red trunks with a white strip. Ali also had red tassels on his boxing shoes. Frazier entered the ring wearing green paisley style trunks, with a stoic look on his face. Frank Sinatra was at ringside as a photographer for Life magazine and Burt Lancaster was part of the closed-circuit broadcast team

Arthur Mercante was the referee when the bell rang for the first round. Ali came out dancing at the sound of the first bell, with his red tassels flying in the air. Ali took the first two rounds simply by boxing, and moving as Frazier followed him around the ring, throwing very few punches. Frazier began to open up in the third round, and began to slow Ali down with body punches in the 6th, 7th, and 8th rounds

Ali rebounded to take round 9 with some beautiful boxing but Frazier was not to be denied on this night, and he was back in control by round 10 as Ali continued to clown and give away rounds during the fight. Frazier seriously hurt Ali in the 11th round, and he was lucky to survive the round. Frazier continued to apply pressure in the 12th and 13th rounds, while Ali continued to fight back in spurts.

Ali gave it all he had left in the 14th round, and he won it by a slight margin. Frazier charged out in the 15th and final round and dropped Ali with a perfectly timed left hook to the jaw. Ali was up before the 10-count with the right side of his jaw swollen. Ali fought back until the final bell in what was a great night of boxing.

Frazier was given a well-deserved unanimous decision by the judges in a very competitive fight. Both fighters' faces were swollen and Frazier was taken to the hospital after the fight for observation. I remember this fight well because at the time of the fight, I was a poor college student, listening to the fight on the radio with other college students.

When I was finally able to watch a tape of the fight, I scored it for Frazier 8-6-1 in rounds, and had him winning by 3 points, as I gave him a 2-point margin for the 15th round knockdown. Ali would go on to defeat Frazier twice in the 1970's, but this night belonged to Joe Frazier.

The Ali vs. Frazier 3 fight in Manila in 1975 may have been a more bitterly contested struggle, but the Frazier vs. Ali 1 fight truly captured a worldwide audience as the true "Fight of the Century".

Bibliography

Information from the following publications was used in preparation for this book.

The Ring magazine, October of 1954 issue

The Ring magazine, December of 1956 issue

The Ring magazine, May of 1974 issue

World Boxing magazine, January of 1976 issue

The Ring magazine, February of 1976 issue

The Ring magazine, March of 1976 issue

World Champion magazine, May of 1977 issue

International Boxing magazine, June of 1978

Guantes magazine, October of 1978

Guantes magazine, Special Edition 1978

Big Book of Boxing, May 1980 issue

Boxing Illustrated magazine, November 1981 issue

Boxing Update magazine, March 10, 1995 issue

The Greatest Champion That Never Was by Jaclyn Weldon White, Mercer University Press 2011

IBRO Journal, issue 132, December 2016

Bibliography (cont.)

Berisha, Visar & Liss et al., *Float Like a Butterfly Sting Like a Bee: Changes in Speech Preceded Parkinsonism Diagnosis for Muhammad Ali.* (Interspeech.2017).

Acknowledgements

This book would not have been possible without the help and guidance of the following people in alphabetical order:

Richard L. Baca, technical support and research

Dr. Rita B. Bermudez, Medical research

Dan Cuoco. Hall of Fame boxing selections

Dean Lingenfelter, Chief editor

Chad Weaver, Boxing records verification

The Front cover photographs are from BoxRec and the Back cover photograph came from Newsday by Dick Morseman.

About the Author

The author, Larry Carli, is a retired Sheriff Detective and District Attorney Criminal Investigator from Sacramento County, California. He has published two books titled "The Illinois Thunderbolt", the life story of boxer Billy Papke, and "The Top Ten Middleweight Champions of All Time". He has also written freelance boxing stories for International Boxing Research Organization, Boxing Illustrated, Fight Beat, and The Ring magazines.

The author is also a former member of the International Boxing Research Organization, the National Sportscasters and Sportswriters Association, and the California Writers Club.

www.ingramcontent.com/pod-product-compliance
Lightning Source LLC
Chambersburg PA
CBHW052036090426
42739CB00010B/1927